ROUGH GUIDES

T0021808

POCKET **ROUGH GUIDE**
MADRID

written and researched by
SIMON BASKETT

CONTENTS

MADRID

The sunniest, highest and liveliest capital city in Europe, Madrid has a lot to take pride in. Indeed, its inhabitants, the madrileños, are so proud of their city that they modestly declare "de Madrid al cielo": that after Madrid there is only one remaining destination – heaven. While their claim may be open to dispute, this compact, frenetic and fascinating city certainly has bags of appeal and its range of attractions has made it a deservedly popular short-break destination.

Catedral de la Alumdena

King Felipe II plucked Madrid from provincial oblivion when he made it capital of the Spanish empire in 1561. The former garrison town enjoyed an initial Golden Age when literature and the arts flourished, but centuries of decline and political turmoil followed. However, with the death of the dictator Franco in 1975 and the return to democracy the city had a second burst of creativity, *La Movida madrileña*, an outpouring of hedonistic, highly innovative and creative forces embodied by film director Pedro Almodóvar. Since the turn of the new century, Madrid has undergone a major facelift, with the completion of state-of-the-art extensions to the leading museums, the creation of new exhibition spaces, the redevelopment of the river area and the regeneration of some of the historic parts of the centre.

The vast majority of the millions of visitors make a beeline for the Prado, the Reina Sofía and the Thyssen-Bornemisza, three magnificent galleries that give the city a weighty claim to being the "European capital of art". Of equal appeal to football fans is the presence of one of the world's most glamorous and successful clubs, Real Madrid. Aside from

Roy Lichtenstein artwork, Museo Reina Sofía

these heavy hitters, there's also a host of smaller museums, palaces and parks, not to mention some of the best tapas, bars and nightlife in Spain.

Madrid's short but eventful history has left behind a mosaic of traditions, cultures and cuisines, and you soon realize it's the inhabitants who play a big part in the city's appeal. Despite morale-sapping economic difficulties, *madrileños* still retain an almost

When to visit

Traditionally, Madrid has a typical **continental climate**, cold and dry in winter, and hot and dry in summer. There were once two rainy periods, in October/November and any time from late March to early May, but this has become increasingly unpredictable due to climate change. With temperatures soaring to around 40ºC in July and August, the best times to visit are generally **spring** and **autumn**, when the city is pleasantly warm. The short, sharp winter takes many visitors by surprise, but crisp, sunny days with clear blue skies compensate for the drop in temperature.

Although Madrid is increasingly falling into line with other European capitals, many places still shut down in **August** as its inhabitants head for the coast or countryside. Luckily for visitors, and those *madrileños* who choose to remain, sights and museums remain open and nightlife takes on a momentum of its own.

Best places for tapas

There is a vast array of bars in Madrid, serving up tasty tapas: take a stroll around Huertas, La Latina, Chueca and Malasaña and you will stumble on some of the best. A few of our favourites are: *Casa González* (see page 61), *Pez Tortilla* (see page 34 and 88), *Casa Amadeo "Los Caracoles"* (see page 48), *Cervecería Cervantes* (see page 77), *Casa Julio* (see page 87), *Casa del Abuelo* (see page 60) and *Vinos 11 Casa Dani* (see page 49).

insatiable appetite for enjoying themselves, whether it be hanging out in the cafés or on the summer terrazas, packing the lanes of the Rastro flea market, filling the restaurants or playing hard and late in the bars and clubs. The nightlife for which Madrid is renowned is merely an extension of the *madrileño* character and the capital's inhabitants consider other European cities positively dull by comparison with their own. The city centre is a mix of bustling,

labyrinthine streets and peaceful squares, punctuated by historic architectural reminders of the past. As with many of its international counterparts, an influx of fast-food franchises and chain stores has challenged the once dominant local bars and shops, but in making the transition from provincial backwater to major European capital, Madrid has managed to preserve many key elements of its own stylish and quirky identity.

Bar in the Malasaña district

Where to...

Shop

Head for Gran Vía and Calle Preciados if you're looking for department and chain stores and for the streets around Plaza Mayor if you're on the hunt for traditional establishments. For fashion and designer labels, the smartest addresses are in Salamanca, but more alternative designers are in Malasaña and Chueca. Fans of street fashion will like the shops in and around Calle Fuencarral. Most areas of the city have their own *mercados* (indoor food markets), many of which have been given a makeover, but for the classic *madrileño* shopping experience make your way to the flea market in the Rastro on a Sunday.
OUR FAVOURITES: Casa de Diego, see page 56. La Chinata, see page 32. El Flamenco Vive, see page 48.

Eat

Eating out in Madrid is one of the highlights of any visit – from backstreet bars to high-class designer restaurants, and a bewildering range of cuisines encompassing tapas, traditional *madrileño* and Spanish regional dishes. Lunch is taken late, with few *madrileños* starting before 2pm, while dinner won't begin until after 8.30pm. Opening hours can be flexible, with many bars and restaurants closing on Sunday evenings or Monday and for all or part of August. You should spend at least one evening sampling the tapas bars around Santa Ana/Huertas and La Latina. Chueca and Malasaña have some superb traditional bars and bright new restaurants, while Salamanca has fewer bars of note, but some extremely good (and expensive) restaurants.
OUR FAVOURITES: Posada de la Villa, see page 33. La Barraca, see page 85. Xentes, see page 48.

Drink

Madrid is packed with a variety of bars, cafés and terrazas. In fact, they are a central feature of *madrileño* life and hanging out in bars is one of the best, and most pleasant, ways to get the feel of the city and its people. The areas bordering Puerta del Sol, in and around Cava Baja and Plaza Chueca are some of the liveliest, but you can stumble across a great bar in almost every street in the city centre.
OUR FAVOURITES: Almendro 13, see page 34. Café el Espejo, see page 96. Taberna Àngel Sierra, see page 89.

Party

As you'd expect with a city whose inhabitants are known as the "gatos" (the cats), there's a huge variety of nightlife on offer in the Spanish capital. The mainstays of the Madrid scene are the *bares de copas*, which get going around 11pm and stay open till 2am. The flashier *discotecas* are rarely worth investigating until around 1 or 2am, although queues often build up quickly after this time. Alonso Martínez, Argüelles and Moncloa are student hangouts, Salamanca is for the wealthy and chic, while head for Malasaña and Chueca if you want to be at the cutting edge of trendiness. You'll find a more eclectic mix on offer in the streets around Sol and Santa Ana.
OUR FAVOURITES: Joy Madrid, see page 43. Kapital, see page 77. Las Carboneras, see page 35.

Madrid at a glance

Plaza de España and beyond p.100.
Swathes of parkland in Casa de Campo and Parque del Oeste provide respite from the bustling streets of the city centre and are home to landmarks of their own such as the zoo and the Parque de Atracciones.

UNIVERSIDAD

Ministerio
del Aire

Palacio Real and Ópera p.36.
Centred around the monumental triangle of the Royal Palace, Almudena cathedral and opera house, this is one of the most elegant and alluring quarters of the city.

MALASAÑA

Centro
Cultural
Conde
Duque

Museo de
Historía de
Madrid

Parque
del Oeste

Museo
Cerralbo

Edificio
España

PLAZA DE ESPAÑA

Intercambiador
de Príncipe Pío

Senado

Edificio
Capitol

La Encarnación

GRAN VÍA

Palacio
Real

Teatro
Real

ÓPERA
Las Descalzas

SOL

Galería de las
Colecciones
Reales

Catedral de la
Almudena

Casa de
Correos

SAN
AN.

Campo
del Moro

Plaza
Mayor

HUERT.

MADRID DE
LOS AUSTRIAS

Iglesia
Colegiata de
San Isidro

Madrid de los Austrias p.26.
The historic core of Madrid and the most atmospheric part of the city, Madrid de los Austrias is the first stop to head for in the Spanish capital.

LA LATINA

LAVAPIÉS

RASTRO

Mercado
Puerta de Toledo

Nuevos Ministerios

Museo de Ciencias Naturales

0	metres	500
0	yards	500

Museo Sorolla

Salamanca and Paseo de la Castellana p.90.
Smart restaurants, corporate office blocks and designer stores line the streets of this elegant, upmarket district that borders the traffic-choked Paseo de la Castellana.

an Vía, Chueca and Malasaña p.78.
orth of the monumental buildings and opping outlets that line the Gran Vía the characterful *barrios* of Chueca d Malasaña.

N

Sol, Santa Ana and Huertas p.50.
The bustling heart of Madrid is centred around the tourist magnet of Plaza de Santa Ana and Calle Huertas.

seo del manticismo

Biblioteca Nacional & Museo del Libro

Las Salesas Reales

SALAMANCA

Museo Arqueológico Nacional

HUECA

Palacio de Buenavista

RETIRO

Palacio de Cibeles

Paseo del Arte and Retiro p.64.
Three world-class art galleries – the Prado, the Thyssen-Bornemisza and the Reina Sofía – all lie within a stone's throw of each other in this chic district that is also bordered by the delightful urban green space of the Retiro Park and the adjoining botanical gardens.

Museo Thyssen

Museo del Prado

Palacio de Cristal

P a r q u e   d e l   R e t i r o

LAS CORTES

CaixaForum

onvento de anta Isabel

Museo Reina Sofía

Rastro, Lavapiés and Embajadores p.44.
Low on sights, but high on atmosphere and full of lively bars and restaurants, this is Madrid's most cosmopolitan neighbourhood.

Estación de Atocha

15

Things not to miss

It's not possible to see everything that Madrid has to offer in one trip – and we don't suggest you try. What follows is a selective taste of the city's highlights, from museums to the best places to eat.

> **Tapas**
See pages 60 and 28
For an authentic night out eating tapas, copy the locals and go bar-hopping in Huertas or La Latina.

< **Museo Thyssen-Bornemisza**
See page 69
A superb collection of art put together by the Thyssen family and which acts as a marvellous complement to the Prado.

∨ **Museo del Prado**
See page 64
Quite simply one of the greatest art museums in the world.

‹ Palacio Real
See page 36
A sumptuous royal palace reflecting the past glories of the Spanish monarchy.

⌄ Plaza Mayor
See page 26
Tucked in behind Calle Mayor, this stunning arcaded plaza is the beating heart of the old city with its cafés, bars, restaurants, buskers, caricaturists and mime artists.

< **Estadio Santiago Bernabéu**
See page 94
The Galácticos may have gone, but this magnificent cathedral of football merits a visit, especially if you can enjoy a game.

∨ **La Galería de las Colecciones Reales**
See page 39
A stunning new museum showcasing the magnificent treasures of the Habsburg and Bourbon dynasties.

∧ The Rastro
See page 45
Chaotic, ramshackle and thorougly enjoyable street market that is a Sunday tradition for many *madrileños*.

< Museo Reina Sofía
See page 68
An essential stop on the Madrid art circuit, the Reina Sofía is home to Picasso's iconic masterpiece *Guernica*.

∧ Clubbing

See page 7

Madrid has a massive range of clubs, from unpretentious *bares de copas* to serious cutting-edge dance venues.

∨ Museo Arqueológico Nacional

See page 90

A formidable collection of Visigothic, Roman, Greek and Egyptian finds in a beautifully imposing refurbished building next to Plaza Colón.

∧ Museo Sorolla
See page 91
The life and works of Spanish artist Joaquín Sorolla housed in his beautiful former residence.

< The Retiro
See page 70
This city-centre park has become *madrileños*' favourite playground with a boating lake, bandstands and a crystal palace housing regular exhibitions.

< **Café culture**
See page 96
Watch the world go by and get a proper cup of coffee at one of the city's traditional cafés.

∨ **Toledo**
See page 113
Packed full of extraordinary sights, Toledo is one of Spain's great historic cities, and the best day-trip from Madrid.

Day one in Madrid

The Prado. See page 64. The Prado contains a fabulous array of masterpieces by artistic greats such as Bosch, El Greco, Titian, Rubens, Velázquez and Goya.

The Retiro. See page 70. Ward off any museum fatigue by freshening up with a stroll around beautiful Retiro park.

🍴 **Lunch**. See page 33. For a taste of some classic Castilian cuisine served up in elegant surroundings, try the well-regarded *Posada de la Villa* on C/ Cava Baja.

Antique store in La Latina

The Palacio Real. See page 36. Marvel at the magnificent, over-the-top decor in this one-time royal residence now used only for ceremonial purposes.

☕ **Coffee**. See page 42. Looking out over the plaza towards the royal palace, the elegant *Café de Oriente* makes a great place for a relaxing drink.

Plaza Mayor. See page 26. Built when the city became Spain's capital in the sixteenth century, Madrid's atmospheric main square retains an aura of traditional elegance.

Madrid de los Austrias. See page 26. Take a step back in time and explore the twisting streets of ancient Madrid around La Latina.

Plaza Mayor

🍴 **Dinner**. See page 60. Hit the tapas trail around Huertas. Hop from bar to bar, sampling local specialities. *Casa Alberto*, *Casa González* and *Casa del Abuelo II* are good places to make a start.

Flamenco. See page 63. Finish the night off with some authentic flamenco at *Cardamomo*.

Flamenco dancer

Day two in Madrid

The Thyssen. See page 69. An outstanding art collection assembled by the Thyssen-Bornemisza dynasty and providing an unprecedented excursion through Western art.

The Santiago Bernabéu. See page 94. Home to the all-star Real Madrid, a tour of this awesome stadium is a must for any football fan. Better still, take in a game.

🍴 **Lunch**. See page 34. Prepare yourself for a spot of shopping in Chueca and Malasaña after sampling some tasty tapas at *Pez Tortilla*.

Shopping. See page 83. Chueca and Malasaña are home to some of the city's hippest fashion outlets and most interesting independent stores.

Museo Reina Sofía. See page 68. An impressive home for Spain's collection of contemporary art, worth the visit if only to see Picasso's *Guernica*.

Gourmet Experience. See page 87. Take in some of the best views in Madrid from the terrace bars on the ninth floor of El Corte Inglés in Callao.

🍴 **Dinner**. See page 32. *El Botín* is reputedly the oldest *meson* in the city and serves up superb, traditional Castilian food.

Club. See page 43. Work off some calories with a dance at one of Madrid's clubs. *Joy Madrid* has an eclectic mix of music, a fun atmosphere and is a fantastic setting for a late-night drink.

The Thyssen

Bookshop in Malaseña

Rooftop bar, El Corte Inglés

Budget Madrid

Many of Madrid's biggest sights are free at certain times, while others charge no entry fee at all. It's possible to spend a great day without paying for anything except food and drink.

Museo de San Isidro. See page 31. Housed in a sixteenth-century mansion that was supposedly once home to the city's patron saint, this museum traces the early history of the Spanish capital.

Museo de Historia de Madrid. See page 82. With an intriguing collection, you can get a rundown of the history of the city at this free museum.

Museo de Historia de Madrid

Lunch. See page 48. With a great value three-course set lunch menu, *La Sanabresa* is one of the best-value local restaurants.

Palacio Real. See page 36. The sumptuous royal palace allows free access for a couple of hours during the afternoon from Monday to Thursday – be prepared to queue.

Templo de Debod. See page 105. Shipped stone by stone from the banks of the River Nile, this ancient Egyptian temple is an incongruous sight in the city. The little exhibition inside is free.

Templo de Debod

The Prado. See page 64. Head here between 6 and 8pm on weekdays (Sun 5–7pm) and you'll see a rare collection of art for nothing.

The Retiro. See page 70. Take a stroll by the lake in the Retiro park to relax and unwind.

Dinner. See page 49. Spoil yourself with the great-value *raciones* and toasted sandwiches at *Melo's* in Lavapiés.

Río Manzanares. See page 106. Finish off the evening with a stroll by the redeveloped river area by the Puente de Segovia.

The Retiro

Off-the-beaten-track Madrid

If you've got the time and have done the big sights, then why not take a break from the crowds and seek out some of Madrid's lesser-known, but highly rewarding attractions.

Monasterio de las Descalzas Reales. See page 41. Hidden behind an innocuous-looking door, this sixteenth-century convent is brimming full of artistic treasures.

San Francisco el Grande. See page 31. Limited opening hours mean that this magnificent church and its frescoes are often overlooked.

Campo del Moro. See page 39. Surprisingly under-visited, this English-style park below the Palacio Real provides a verdant retreat away from the bustle of the nearby streets.

Museo de Cerralbo. See page 101. A charming museum housed in a beautifully restored mansion, home to the eclectic treasures of the nineteenth-century aristocrat, Marqués de Cerralbo.

Lunch. See page 88. Tucked away in the backstreets north of Gran Vía, *Pez Gordo* serves a fabulous range of tapas and beer at reasonable prices.

Museo Nacional del Romanticismo. See page 82. This delightful museum recreates bourgeois life in nineteenth-century Madrid.

Museo Sorolla. See page 91. The artist's elegant former home provides the perfect setting for his luminescent paintings.

Museo Lázaro Galdiano. See page 91. Well off the tourist trail, this former private collection gets less than its fair share of attention and yet it houses an amazing cornucopia of art treasures.

Dinner. See page 109. Try out some no-nonsense Asturian cooking at *La Pomarada* on Calle Conde Duque.

Monasterio de las Descalzas Reales

Campo del Moro

Museo de Cerralbo

Kids' Madrid

Although it may not be able to boast the major child-oriented sights of some big cities, there is plenty to keep the kids entertained for a short stay in the Spanish capital.

The Teleférico. See page 105. For a bird's-eye view of the city, take the cable car across the Manzanares river to Casa de Campo.

Zoo-Aquarium. See page 106. The Casa de Campo is home to an engaging zoo, complete with lions, bears, pandas, sharks and an extensive collection of reptiles.

Parque de Atracciones. See page 107. If the zoo doesn't appeal, there is a popular theme park alongside with a vast range of dizzying rides catering for all ages.

Lunch. See page 110. Next to the lake in Casa de Campo *El Urogallo* has great views and is a good bet after a zoo or amusement park trip.

The Teleférico

The Retiro. See page 70. The Retiro park has plenty of child-friendly attractions including play areas, puppet shows, duck ponds and a boating lake.

Museo de Ferrocarril. See page 47. With its model railways and array of full-size locomotives, this museum will be a hit with most children – and their parents too.

Museo de Cera. See page 91. Less parochial than it once was, there are now enough international figures and sports stars in the city's wax museum to interest most children, though many only bear a passing resemblance to the real thing.

Bengal tiger, Zoo-Aquarium

Dinner. See page 99. The *Lateral* chain of tapas bars has a big enough menu and a relaxed, modern vibe that make it a good place to head with the kids.

Finish the evening with a visit to the visually impressive Nomad Museo (see page 101) and its immersive digital technology experiences.

Frog statue, Plaza de Colón

Green Madrid

Despite the hustle and bustle of the city centre, Madrid is home to some appealing green spaces that provide visitors with a chance to relax, unwind and recharge their batteries.

Campo del Moro. See page 39. For the best views of the Royal Palace head for an early morning stroll along the shady paths of one of Madrid's most beautiful and underused parks.

Casa de Campo. See page 106. Once part of the royal hunting estate, Casa de Campo is the biggest and wildest of the city's parks.

Lunch. See page 109. Nothing better than a spot of roast chicken and cider after a morning stroll at *Casa Mingo* – a spit-and-sawdust eatery – close to Parque del Oeste.

Campo del Moro

Parque del Oeste. See page 105. This lovely park contains assorted statues, a fragrant rose garden and even a genuine Egyptian temple. Offers some great views over Casa de Campo and out towards the mountains too.

CaixaForum Vertical Garden. See page 71. A stunning vertical garden, designed by French botanist Patrick Blanc, adorns the wall outside this innovative exhibition space.

Jardines Botánicos. See page 71. Dating back to the eighteenth century, the botanical gardens form an amazingly tranquil oasis in the city.

CaixaForum Vertical Garden

The Retiro. See page 70. The city-centre park has become the *madrileños* favourite playground with plenty of routes for runners, a boating lake, and a crystal palace hosting regular exhibitions.

Dinner. See page 76. *Taberna Pedraza* is the perfect place to sample some quality tapas after an evening stroll in the Retiro.

Jardines Botánicos

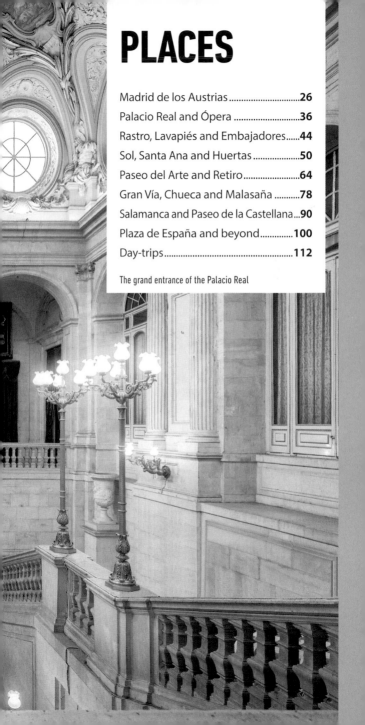

PLACES

The grand entrance of the Palacio Real

Madrid de los Austrias

Named after the dynasty that once ruled Spain, the district known as Madrid de los Austrias, or Habsburg Madrid, is made up of some of the oldest and most atmospheric parts of the city. Centred around the extravagant Plaza Mayor, the area is a twisting grid of streets, filled with Flemish-inspired architecture of red brick and grey stone. Most visitors only make it to the Plaza Mayor and its over-priced cafés and restaurants, but there are appealing sights scattered throughout the area, especially in the barrio (district) of La Latina, which stretches south of the square. This region is also home to some of the city's best restaurants, tapas bars and flamenco tablaos, especially around calles Almendro, Cava Baja and Cava Alta.

Plaza Mayor

MAP PAGE 28, POCKET MAP C12

Ⓜ Sol.

The splendidly theatrical Plaza Mayor was originally the brainchild of Felipe II who, in the late sixteenth century, wished to construct a more prestigious focus for his new capital. The Casa de la Panadería on the north side of the square is the oldest building, dating from 1590, but, like much of the plaza, was rebuilt after fires in the seventeenth and eighteenth centuries. The gaudy frescoes that adorn the facade were only added in 1992. It now houses the municipal tourist office (daily 9.30am–8.30pm).

Plaza de la Villa

Capable of holding up to fifty thousand people, the square was used for state occasions, *autos-de-fé* (public trials of heretics followed, usually, by burning of the victims), plays and bullfights. The large bronze equestrian statue in the middle is of Felipe III and dates from 1616. During the Second Republic an explosive blew a hole in the statue scattering hundreds of tiny bone fragments from the sparrows that had got stuck inside after they had flown into the horse's mouth. The mouth has since been sealed.

Today, Plaza Mayor is primarily a tourist haunt, full of expensive outdoor cafés and restaurants. However, an air of grandeur clings to the plaza and it still hosts public functions, from outdoor theatre and music to Christmas fairs and a Sunday stamp and coin market.

Calle Mayor

MAP PAGE 28, POCKET MAP A12–D12
Ⓜ **Sol.**

One of the oldest thoroughfares in the city, Calle Mayor was for centuries the route for religious processions from the Palacio Real to the Monastery of Los Jerónimos. The street is now home to some rather tacky souvenir shops and bars, but it is flanked by the facades of some of the most evocative buildings in the city. Set back from the road, near the entrance to the Plaza Mayor, is the splendid decorative ironwork of the **Mercado de San Miguel** (Sun–Thurs 10am–midnight, Fri–Sat 10am–1am; Ⓦ mercadodesanmiguel. es; see page 34). Built in 1916, it was formerly one of the old-style food markets scattered throughout the city, but it has now been refurbished and converted into a stylish tourist-oriented emporium complete with oyster and champagne bar. Further down the street at No 69 is the **Centro Sefardí-Israel** (Mon–Fri 10.30am–8pm, Sat & Sun 10.30–2.30pm; Ⓦ sefarad-israel. es; free), which stages cultural events and exhibitions.

Calle Mayor

San Nicolás de los Servitas

MAP PAGE 28, POCKET MAP A12
Plaza de San Nicolás 1 Mon–Sat 8.30–9.30am & 7–8.30pm, Sun 10am–1.45pm & 6.30–8.45pm. Ⓜ **Ópera.**

Largely rebuilt between the fifteenth and seventeenth centuries, Madrid's oldest church still includes a twelfth-century Mudéjar tower featuring traditional Arabic horseshoe arches. Juan de Herrera, architect of El Escorial (see page 119), was buried in the crypt though his remains were later moved.

Plaza de la Villa

MAP PAGE 28, POCKET MAP A12
Ⓜ **Sol.**

This charming plaza, just off Calle Mayor, showcases three centuries of Spanish architectural development. The oldest buildings are the simple but eye-catching fifteenth-century **Torre y Casa de Los Lujanes**, where Francis I of France is said to have been imprisoned by Emperor Charles V after the Battle of Pavia in 1525. On the south side of the square is the **Casa de Cisneros**, constructed for the nephew of Cardinal Cisneros (early sixteenth-century Inquisitor-General and

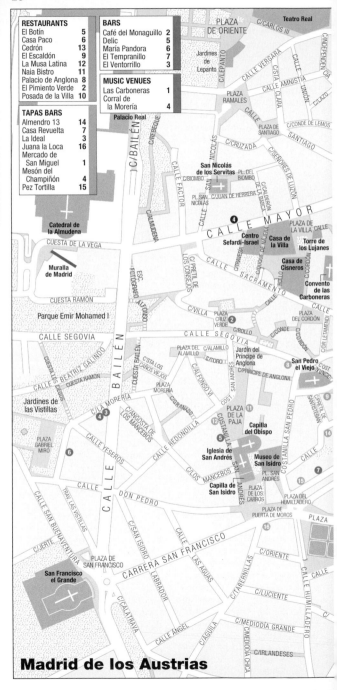

RESTAURANTS

El Botín	5
Casa Paco	6
Cedrón	13
El Escaldón	9
La Musa Latina	12
Naia Bistro	11
Palacio de Anglona	8
El Pimiento Verde	2
Posada de la Villa	10

TAPAS BARS

Almendro 13	14
Casa Revuelta	7
La Ideal	3
Juana la Loca	16
Mercado de San Miguel	1
Mesón del Champiñón	4
Pez Tortilla	15

BARS

Café del Monaguillo	2
Delic	5
María Pandora	6
El Tempranillo	7
El Ventorrillo	3

MUSIC VENUES

Las Carboneras	1
Corral de la Morería	4

Madrid de los Austrias

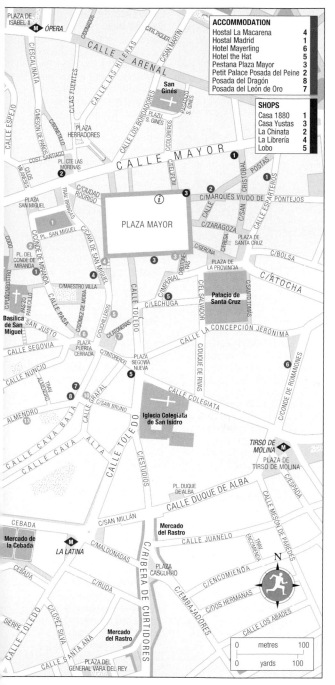

ACCOMMODATION

Hostal La Macarena	4
Hostal Madrid	1
Hotel Mayerling	6
Hotel the Hat	5
Pestana Plaza Mayor	3
Petit Palace Posada del Peine	2
Posada del Dragón	8
Posada del León de Oro	7

SHOPS

Casa 1880	1
Casa Yustas	3
La Chinata	2
La Librería	4
Lobo	5

Parque Emir Mohamed I

Convento de las Carboneras

MAP PAGE 28, POCKET MAP B13
Plaza Conde de Miranda 3. Church: Mon–
Sat 8.30am–1pm & 4.30–7.30pm, Sun
9.30am–1pm & 4.30–7.30pm. Ⓜ Sol.
Founded in the early seventeenth
century, this convent belongs to
the closed Hieronymite Order. It's
famous for its home-made biscuits
and cakes – a tradition in Spanish
convents since the time of St Teresa
of Ávila, who gave out sweetened
egg yolks to the poor – which can be
purchased every day (9.30am–1pm
& 4.30–6.15pm; closed August).
Ring the bell above the sign reading
venta de dulces to be let in, then
follow the signs to the *torno*; the
business takes place by means of
a revolving drum to preserve the
closed nature of the order.

Regent of Spain) in the intricate
Plateresque style.

The **Casa de la Villa** occupies
the remaining side. An emblem of
Habsburg Madrid, it was constructed
in fits and starts from the mid-
seventeenth century to house the
offices and records of the council,
who have since moved on to more
grandiloquent headquarters in the
Palacio de Cibeles. The initial design
by Juan Gómez de Mora wasn't
completed until 1693, 45 years after
his death, and was mellowed by the
addition of Baroque details in the
eighteenth century.

Parque Emir Mohamed I

MAP PAGE 28, POCKET MAP B6
Sat, Sun and holidays 10am–9pm. Ⓜ Ópera.
It is easy to miss this small, enclosed
park opposite the crypt of the
Almudena cathedral, but it is notable
for the fragments of the city walls
that date back to the ninth and
twelfth centuries. The park lies on
the Cuesta de la Vega, former site of
one of the main entrances to Muslim
Madrid, while nearby, the narrow,
labyrinthine streets of the former
Moorish quarter, La Morería, are still
clearly laid out on medieval lines.

Basílica de San Miguel

MAP PAGE 28, POCKET MAP B13
C/San Justo 4. July–Sept Mon–Sat 9.45am–
1pm & 6–9.15pm, Sun 9.45am–1.30pm
& 6.30–9.15pm; Oct–June Mon–Sat
9.45am–1.15pm & 5.30–9.15pm, Sun
9.45am–2.15pm & 6–9.15pm. Ⓦ basilicade
sanmiguel.org. Ⓜ La Latina or Sol.
Standing among a host of other
graceful buildings – most of
which house local government
offices – San Miguel stands out
as one of the few examples of a
full-blown Baroque church in
Madrid. Designed at the end of
the seventeenth century for Don
Luis, the precocious 5-year-old
Archbishop of Toledo and youngest
son of Felipe V, its features include
an unconventional convex facade
with four recesses, each containing
a statue, variously representing
Charity, Strength, Faith and Hope.

San Pedro el Viejo

MAP PAGE 28, POCKET MAP B13
Costanilla de San Pedro. Mon–Thurs & Sat
9am–12.30pm & 6–9pm, Fri 7am–9pm, Sun
9am–12.30pm. Ⓜ La Latina.
At the heart of busy La Latina is
the Mudéjar tower of San Pedro El
Viejo. The second-oldest church

in Madrid, it's said to have been founded in the fourteenth century by Alfonso XI, and stands on the site of an old mosque, though most of the church was rebuilt in the seventeenth century.

Plaza de la Paja

MAP PAGE 28, POCKET MAP A14
Ⓜ La Latina.

One of the real gems of old Madrid, this ancient sloping plaza was the commercial and civic hub of the city before the construction of the Plaza Mayor, and was once surrounded by a series of mansions owned by local dignitaries. With the restored houses beaming down on the former market square, this is a rare peaceful and traffic-free spot in the city. At the bottom is the pretty little Jardin del Príncipe de Anglona (daily: summer 10am–10pm; winter 10am–6.30pm), a survivor of the gardens that used to be attached to the nearby mansions.

Iglesia de San Andrés, Capilla del Obispo and Capilla de San Isidro

MAP PAGE 28, POCKET MAP A14
Plaza de San Andrés. Mon–Fri & Sat 9am–1pm & 6–8pm, Sun 10am–1pm (currently closed for restoration). Ⓜ La Latina.

The Iglesia de San Andrés was badly damaged by an anarchist attack in 1936, and the adjoining Gothic Capilla del Obispo (guided tours Tues 10am, 10.45am & 11.30am; Thurs 4 & 4.45pm, closed July & Aug; reservation only on ☎ 915 592 874 or through the cathedral museum; charge), with its polychromed altarpiece and alabaster tombs, was reopened in 2012 following a forty-year restoration. The main church and the Baroque Capilla de San Isidro are reached by walking round the building into Plaza de San Andrés. The chapel was built in the mid-seventeenth century to hold the remains of Madrid's patron saint, San Isidro (since moved to the Iglesia de San Isidro), and

the interior features a beautifully sculpted dome.

Museo de San Isidro

MAP PAGE 28, POCKET MAP B7
Plaza de San Andrés 2. mid-June to mid-Sept Tues–Fri 10am-7pm; mid-Sept to mid-June Tues–Fri 10am-8pm. Free. Ⓦ madrid.es/museosanisidro. Ⓜ La Latina.

Housed in a reconstructed sixteenth-century mansion – supposedly home to Madrid's patron saint San Isidro – this museum includes an exhibition on the history of the Spanish capital. The city's archeological collection is in the basement, while the rest of the building is given over to the saint himself, with displays relating to his life and miraculous activities. The house also contains a well, site of one of Isidro's most famous exploits: he rescued his young son from the murky depths, by praying until the waters rose to the surface. The seventeenth-century chapel contained within the museum is built on the spot where the saint was said to have died in 1172.

San Francisco el Grande

MAP PAGE 28, POCKET MAP B7
Plaza de San Francisco 11. Tues–Sat 10.30am–12.30pm & 4–5.30pm, July & Aug Tues–Fri 10.30am–12.30pm. Charge, including guided tour; free on Thurs. Ⓜ La Latina.

Following a twenty-year restoration programme, you can appreciate this magnificent eighteenth-century domed church in something close to its original glory. Inside, each of the six chapels is designed in a distinct style ranging from Mozarabic and Renaissance to Baroque and Neoclassical. Look out for the early Goya, *The Sermon of San Bernadino of Siena*, in the chapel on your immediate left as you enter, which contains a self-portrait of the 37-year-old artist (in the yellow suit on the right).

Even if your Spanish is not that good, follow the guided tour to get a glimpse of the church's other art treasures, including paintings by José de Ribera and Zurbarán.

Shops

Casa 1880

MAP PAGE 28, POCKET MAP C12
C/Mayor 9. ⓦ turron1880.com. ⓜ Sol.
One for the sweet-toothed, this shop specializes in the Spanish delicacies of *turrón* (nougat), *mazapan* (marzipan) and *polvorones* (small crumbly shortbread-like sweets). Every imaginable type of *turrón* is available, from the traditional creamy variety from Jijona and crunchy classic from Alicante to new flavours such as tiramisu and chocolate and pink gin.

Casa Yustas

MAP PAGE 28, POCKET MAP C12
Plaza Mayor 30 ⓦ casayustas.com. ⓜ Sol.
Established back in 1886, Madrid's oldest hat shop sells every conceivable model from pith helmets and commando berets to panamas and bowlers. There's also a large range of souvenir-style goods, including Lladró porcelain figurines.

La Chinata

MAP PAGE 28, POCKET MAP B12
C/Mayor 44 ⓦ lachinata.es. ⓜ Sol.

A wonderful selection of pure and flavoured olive oils on offer, from top quality *virgen extra* to varieties containing a touch of garlic, chili, basil and lemon. Other gourmet products ranging from flavoured vinegars and honey to cheese, olives and stuffed peppers are also available at this delightful extremeño business.

La Librería

MAP PAGE 28, POCKET MAP A12
C/Mayor 8 ⓦ edicioneslalibreria.es. ⓜ Sol.
Tiny place full of books just about Madrid. Most are in Spanish, but many would serve as coffee-table souvenirs. Also good for old prints of the city.

Lobo

MAP PAGE 28, POCKET MAP C13
C/Toledo 30 ⓦ calzadoslobo.com.
ⓜ La Latina.
Great old-fashioned shoe shop, with anything from espadrilles to Menorcan sandals in every conceivable colour. Excellent for kids' shoes.

Restaurants

El Botín

MAP PAGE 28, POCKET MAP B13
C/Cuchilleros 17 ⓦ botin.es. ⓜ Sol.
Established in 1725, the atmospheric *El Botín* is cited in the *Guinness Book of Records* as Europe's oldest restaurant. Favoured by Hemingway, it's inevitably a tourist haunt, but not such a bad one. Highlights are the Castilian roasts – especially *cochinillo* (suckling pig) and *cordero lechal* (lamb). €€€

Casa Paco

MAP PAGE 28, POCKET MAP B13
Plaza Puerta Cerrada 11 ⓦ casapaco1933.es.
ⓜ La Latina.
This classic, traditional *comedor*, with no-nonsense service, dishes out some of the best meat dishes in town. Specializes in sirloin steak (*solomillo*), and another delicious cut known as *cebón de buey*. The home-made tortilla is also excellent. €€

Roasting *cochinillo* at El Botín

Cedrón

MAP PAGE 28, POCKET MAP B14
C/Almendro 25 Ⓦ cedron.es. Ⓜ La Latina.
Spanish/Argentine restaurant and
wine bar housed in a beautiful old
building in the heart of La Latina.
The brief, but carefully selected
menu includes *ceviche frito*, cod
croquetas and Argentine steaks. €€

El Escaldón

MAP PAGE 28, POCKET MAP B14
C/Nuncio 17 Ⓦ elscaldon.com. Ⓜ La Latina.
Cuisine from the Canary Islands in
this friendly, good-value restaurant
in a quiet spot in La Latina. Starters
include *ropa vieja* (strips of meat
and vegetables) and *papas arrugadas*
(potatoes smothered in spicy sauce
and coriander), while the tuna
and spicy chicken are among the
standout mains. €€

La Musa Latina

MAP PAGE 28, POCKET MAP A14
Costanilla San Andrés 12 Ⓦ grupolamusa.com.
Ⓜ La Latina.
Stylish place serving a great-value
menú del día (check the website
for what's on offer each day), and a
selection of modern tapas such as
langoustine and avocado tempura,
venison in whiskey sauce and wok
dishes. It has a popular summer terrace
on the plaza and cool brick-walled bar
downstairs with DJ sessions. €

Naia Bistro

MAP PAGE 28, POCKET MAP A14
Plaza de la Paja 3 Ⓦ naiabistro.com. Ⓜ La Latina.
Relaxed restaurant with light, airy
decor serving up well-presented,
creative cuisine in a fine setting on
an ancient plaza. Starters include
anchovies with sun-dried tomatoes
and jalapeño pepper; mains such
as baby squid with lemon *alioli* are
also tempting. €€

Palacio de Anglona

MAP PAGE 28, POCKET MAP A13
C/Segovia 13 Ⓦ palaciodeanglona.com.
Ⓜ La Latina.
Modern, minimalist decor in this
good-value restaurant housed in the

Mushroom tapas

cellars of an old La Latina mansion.
Mains include smoked salmon with
mango and seaweed, steak tartar,
and a selection of Mediterranean
rice dishes. Cocktails are served in
the lounge bar. €€

El Pimiento Verde

MAP PAGE 28, POCKET MAP A13
C/Conde de Miranda 4 Ⓦ elpimientoverde.
com. Ⓜ Ópera or Sol.
Basque restaurant just behind the
Mercado de San Miguel serving up
some high quality meat, fish and
traditional stews. The *chipirones
rellenos en su tinta* (stuffed baby
squid in their own ink) and
the *solomillo* (sirloin steak) are
highlights. An excellent selection of
wines too. Closed August. €€€

Posada de la Villa

MAP PAGE 28, POCKET MAP B14
C/Cava Baja 9 Ⓦ posadadelavilla.com.
Ⓜ La Latina.
La Latina's most attractive
restaurant, spread over three
floors of a seventeenth-century
inn. Cooking is *madrileño*,
including superb roast lamb,
which is the house speciality.
Closed August. €€€

Jamón ibérico on sale at a market stall

Tapas bars

Almendro 13

MAP PAGE 28, POCKET MAP B14
C/Almendro 13 Ⓦ almendro13.com.
Ⓜ La Latina.

Packed at weekends, this fashionable wood-panelled bar serves great *fino* sherry and house specials of *huevos rotos* (fried eggs on a bed of crisps) and *roscas relleñas* (bread rings stuffed with various meats). €

Casa Revuelta

MAP PAGE 28, POCKET MAP C13
C/Latoneros 3 Ⓦ casarevuelta.com.
Ⓜ Sol or La Latina.

A timeless, tiny, down-to-earth bar located in an alleyway just south of Plaza Mayor. It serves a melt-in-the-mouth tapa of *bacalao frito* (battered cod). Closed August. €

La Ideal

MAP PAGE 28, POCKET MAP C13
C/Botoneras 4 Ⓦ facebook.com/bar.la.ideal.
Ⓜ Sol.

Queues are normally spilling out the door on this popular tiny corridor bar just off Plaza Mayor, which specializes in *bocadillos de* *calamares* washed down with a beer, but service is super efficient and the turnover is quick, so don't be put off. The next door bar *La Campana* also offers a similar deal. €

Juana la Loca

MAP PAGE 28, POCKET MAP C7
Plaza Puerta de Moros 4
Ⓦ juanalalocamadrid.com. Ⓜ La Latina.

Fashionable hangout on the edge of the square serving inventive *raciones* – *tortilla* with caramelized onion, tuna tartar with wasabi – and a great selection of very tasty, but fairly pricey, *pintxos*. Closed August. €€

Mercado de San Miguel

MAP PAGE 28, POCKET MAP B12
Plaza de San Miguel
Ⓦ mercadodesanmiguel.es. Ⓜ Sol.

Transformed from a neighbourhood market into a hip location for an *aperitivo*, this beautiful wrought-iron *mercado* is worth exploring at almost any time of day. There's something for everyone, from vermouth and champagne to salt cod, oysters and sushi. €€

Mesón del Champiñón

MAP PAGE 28, POCKET MAP B13
Cava de San Miguel 17
Ⓦ mesondelchampinon.com. Ⓜ Sol.

Traditional cellar tavern close to Plaza Mayor, rightly renowned for its signature mushroom tapa. The *pimientos de Padrón*, *calamares* and *croquetas* are good too. Touristy but friendly service and a fun atmosphere. €

Pez Tortilla

MAP PAGE 28, POCKET MAP A14
C/Cava Baja 42 Ⓦ peztortilla.com. Ⓜ La Latina.

Delicious *tortillas* and *croquetas* in this pint-sized bar on the bustling Cava Baja. Not only can you order the classic *tortilla*, but there are other tasty variations such as parmesan with basil and sun-dried tomato, goat's cheese with caramelised onion, or *morcilla* (blood sausage). €

Bars

Café del Monaguillo

MAP PAGE 28, POCKET MAP A13
Plaza Cruz Verde 3 bit.ly/CafeMonaguillo.
⓶ La Latina.

Relaxed café-bar in a small plaza
tucked into the side of Calle
Segovia. Inside its bookshop-like
interior are some comfy sofas, while
outside there is a great terrace. A
great place to chill out just a stone's
throw from the busy centre.

Delic

MAP PAGE 28, POCKET MAP A14
Costanilla San Andrés 14 ⓦdelic.es.
ⓂLa Latina.

Serving home-made cakes, fruit
juices and coffee, this is a pleasant
café by day, offers a decent *menú
del dia* and transforms itself into a
crowded but friendly cocktail bar by
night. Closed first half of August.

María Pandora

MAP PAGE 28, POCKET MAP B7
Plaza Gabriel Miró 1 ⓦmariapandora.com.
ⓂLa Latina or Ópera.

An incongruous mix of
champagnería (champagne bar)
and fin de siècle *café cultural*,
where quality *cava* can be enjoyed
with the perfect accompaniment
of chocolates and mellow jazz.
Opening hours can vary. Closed
second half of August.

El Tempranillo

MAP PAGE 28, POCKET MAP B14
C/Cava Baja 38 ☎913 641 532.
ⓂLa Latina.

Popular little wine bar serving a
vast range of domestic wines by the
glass. A great place to discover your
favourite Spanish *vino* – and the
tapas are excellent too.

El Ventorrillo

MAP PAGE 28, POCKET MAP C7
C/Bailén 14 ☎913 663 578. ⓂLa Latina
or Ópera.

This popular terraza is great for
a relaxing drink while enjoying

the *vistillas* (little views) over the
cathedral and mountains, but avoid
the overpriced tapas.

Music venues

Las Carboneras

MAP PAGE 28, POCKET MAP B13
Plaza Conde de Miranda 1
ⓦtablaolascarboneras.com. ⓂSol.

Geared up for the tourist market,
this *tablao* has gained a decent
reputation on the flamenco scene
with a good range of guest artists.
With two shows nightly (Mon–
Sat), accompanied by either dinner
or a drink, it remains slightly
cheaper than its rivals. Children
8–16 years old are half price.

Corral de la Morería

MAP PAGE 28, POCKET MAP C7
C/Morería 17 ⓦcorraldelamoreria.com.
ⓂLa Latina or Ópera.

A renowned and atmospheric,
if expensive, venue for serious
flamenco acts. There are shows
every evening, but it's double the
price if you want to dine in the
restaurant as well.

Corral de la Morería performance

Palacio Real and Ópera

Although the barrio only became fashionable in the mid-nineteenth century, the attractions found in the compact area around Ópera metro station date back as far as the 1500s. The imposing and suitably lavish Palacio Real (Royal Palace) dominates this part of the city, bordered by the somewhat disappointing Catedral de la Almudena, the new granite slab of a building housing the Galería de las Colecciones Reales (the Royal Collections Gallery), as well as the tranquil gardens of the Campo del Moro. The Teatro Real and Plaza de Oriente bring some nineteenth-century sophistication to the area, while the two monastery complexes of la Encarnación and las Descalzas Reales conceal an astounding selection of artistic delights. For after-dark attractions, the area is home to one of the city's leading clubs as well as a handful of pleasant cafés and restaurants.

Palacio Real

MAP PAGE 38, POCKET MAP B5–C5
C/Bailén. April–Sept Mon–Sat 10am–7pm, Sun 10am–4pm; Oct–March Mon–Sat 10am–6pm, Sun 10am–4pm. Closed for state occasions and holidays. Charge. Ⓦ patrimonionacional.es. Ⓜ Ópera.

Entrance hall, Palacio Real

The present Palacio Real (Royal Palace) was built by Felipe V after the ninth-century Arab-built Alcázar was destroyed by fire in 1734. The Bourbon monarch, who had been brought up in the more luxurious surroundings of Versailles, took the opportunity to replace it with an altogether grander affair. He did not, however, live to see its completion and the palace only became habitable in 1764 during the reign of Carlos III. Nowadays it's used only for ceremonial purposes, with the present royal family preferring the more modest Zarzuela Palace, 15km northwest of the city.

The ostentation lacking in the palace's exterior is more than compensated for inside, with swirling marble floors, celestial frescoes and gold furnishings. It's a flamboyant display of wealth and power that was firmly at odds with Spain's declining status at the time. Look out for the grandiose **Salón del Trono** (Throne Room), the incredible oriental-style **Salón**

Catedral de la Almudena

de Gasparini (the Gasparini Room) and the marvellous **Sala de Porcelan**a (Porcelain Room), decorated with one thousand gold, green and white interlocking pieces.

The palace outbuildings and annexes include the **Armería Real** (Royal Armoury), with its fascinating collection of guns, swords and armour. There's also a laboratory-like eighteenth century **farmacia** (pharmacy) and the refurbished basement **Cocina Real** (Royal Kitchen, extra charge). There is a ceremonial changing of the Royal Guard in the central courtyard at noon on the first Wednesday of the month (except Jan, Aug & Sept; see Ⓦ guardiareal.org for details).

Jardines de Sabatini

MAP PAGE 38, POCKET MAP B4–C4
Daily: May–Sept 9am–10pm; Oct–April 9am–9pm. Ⓜ Ópera.

The Jardines de Sabatini (Sabatini Gardens) make an ideal place from which to view the northern facade of the palace or to watch the sun go down. They contain a small ornamental lake, some fragrant magnolia trees and manicured hedges, while in summer, they're often used as a concert venue.

Catedral de la Almudena

MAP PAGE 38, POCKET MAP B6
Daily: 9am–8pm, July & Aug 10am–9pm. Not open for visits during Mass (Mon–Sat noon, 6pm & 7pm, Sun & holidays noon, 6pm & 7pm; July & Aug noon & 8pm). Free, with voluntary donations. Ⓦ catedraldelaalmudena.es. Ⓜ Ópera.

Planned centuries ago, Madrid's cathedral, Nuestra Señora de la Almudena, was plagued by lack of funds, bombed in the Civil War and finally opened in 1993. In 2004, it was the venue for the wedding of the then heir to the throne, Prince Felipe, and his former newsreader bride, Letizia Ortiz.

The cathedral's cold Gothic interior housed within its stark Neoclassical shell is not particularly inspiring, though the garish ceiling designs and the sixteenth-century altarpiece in the Almudena chapel are exceptions. To one side of the main facade is a small **museum** (Mon–Sat 10am–2.30pm; charge) containing some of the cathedral's treasures, though the main reason

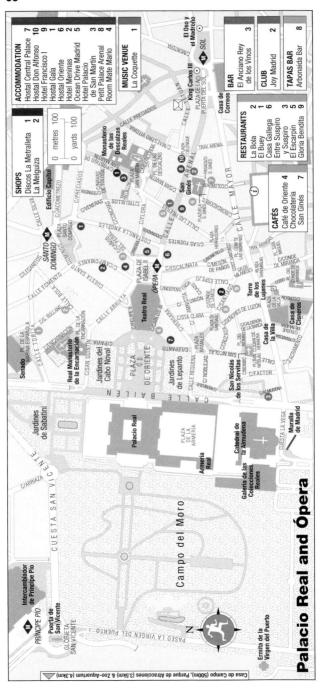

ACCOMMODATION
Hostal Central Palace	7
Hostal Don Alfonso	10
Hotel Francisco I	9
Hostal Gala	1
Hostal Oriente	6
Hotel Meninas	2
Ocean Drive Madrid	5
Hotel Palacio de San Martín	3
Petit Palace Arenal	8
Room Mate Mario	4

MUSIC VENUE
La Coquette	1

BAR
El Anciano Rey de los Vinos	3

CLUB
Joy Madrid	2

TAPAS BAR
Arbonaida Bar	8

SHOPS
Discos La Metralleta	1
La Melguiza	2

RESTAURANTS
La Bola	1
El Buey	6
Casa Gallega	3
Entre Suspiro y Suspiro	5
El Escarpín	9
Gloria Bendita	7

CAFÉS
Café de Oriente	4
Chocolatería San Ginés	7

Palacio Real and Ópera

Casa de Campo (500m), Parque de Atracciones (3.5km) & Zoo-Aquarium (4.3km)

to visit is to gain access to the dome from where you can enjoy some fantastic views over the city. The entrance to the **crypt** (Mon–Fri 10am–2pm & 4.308pm, sat, Sun and holidays 10am–8pm; guided visits Mon–Fri 10am & noon; charge; ⓦ bit.ly/CryptTours) with its forest of columns and dimly lit chapels is on C/Mayor.

La Galería de las Colecciones Reales

MAP PAGE 38, POCKET MAP B6
Mon–Sat 10am–8pm, Sun 10am–7pm.
Charge. ⓦ coleccionesreales.es. Ⓜ Ópera.
This vast new granite block of a building was squeezed in between the Palacio Real and the cathedral to house the hugely impressive collections of art, sculpture, tapestries, armour, carriages and objets d'art belonging to the Habsburg and Bourbon royal dynasties. Over seventeen years in the making, partly because of the complexity of the accompanying archeological excavations of the city walls that lie beneath it, the final outcome is spectacular. Visitors are directed down an enormous internal ramp towards the Austrias

(Habsburg) collection on the floor A and then down to the Bourbons on floor B. Informative videos provide the historical context and the magnificent exhibits are displayed to full effect in the open-plan display halls. Highlights of the collection include a wonderful series of devotional pieces by Juan de Flandes, stunning works by El Greco and Titian, a suit of armour worn by Carlos V, an astonishing Bernini bronze of the crucifixion and Goya's masterfully revealing portraits of Carlos IV and his wife Maria Luisa de Parma. You can access the Campo de Moro as you descend to the lower floor which houses temporary exhibitions and the immersive video experience showcasing the different royal palaces in and around Madrid.

Campo del Moro

MAP PAGE 38, POCKET MAP A4–B6
Entrance on Paseo de la Virgen del Puerto.
Daily: April–Sept 10am–8pm; Oct–March 10am–6pm. Closed occasionally for state occasions. Ⓜ Príncipe Pío.
One of the most underused and beautiful of Madrid's parks, the Campo del Moro gets its name

Campo del Moro

Plaza de Oriente

neo-Fascists still gather here on the anniversary of his death, November 20.

The fountain in the centre was designed by Narciso Pascual y Colomer, who also transferred the bronze equestrian statue of Felipe IV here from the garden of the Buen Retiro Palace, near the Prado. Dating from 1640, this statue is reputedly the first-ever bronze featuring a rearing horse – Galileo is said to have helped with the calculations to make it balance. Other statues depict Spanish kings and queens, and were originally designed to adorn the palace facade, but were too heavy or, according to one version, too ugly, and were removed on the orders of Queen Isabel Farnese.

There's a very French feel to the buildings overlooking the square, with their glass-fronted balconies, underlined by the elegant neo-Baroque *Café de Oriente*, a favourite with the opera crowd.

Teatro Real

MAP PAGE 38, POCKET MAP A11–B11
Plaza de Isabel II Daily 10am–1.30pm; closed August. Ⓦ teatroreal.es. Ⓜ Ópera.

When it opened in 1850, the hulking grey hexagonal opera house became the hub of fashionable Madrid and staged highly successful works by Verdi and Wagner. It fell into decay in the late twentieth century and after a ten-year refurbishment – that should have lasted four – and a staggering US$150 million in costs, it finally reopened in October 1997. With its lavish red and gold decor, crystal chandeliers, state-of-the-art lighting and superb acoustics it makes a truly magnificent setting for opera, ballet and classical concerts. Tickets usually range from €100 to €300, but you'll need to book well in advance for the best seats.

from being the site of the Moors' encampment, from where, in 1109, they mounted their unsuccessful attempt to reconquer Madrid. It later became a venue for medieval tournaments and celebrations. After the building of the Palacio Real several schemes to landscape the area were put forward, but it wasn't until 1842 that things got under way. Based around two monumental fountains, *Las Conchas* and *Los Tritones*, the grassy gardens are very English in style, featuring shady paths and ornamental pools, and provide an excellent refuge from the summer heat, as well as a splendid view of the palace.

Plaza de Oriente

MAP PAGE 38, POCKET MAP A11
Ⓜ Ópera.

The aristocratic, pedestrianized Plaza de Oriente is one of the most attractive open spaces in Madrid. The days when Franco used to address crowds here from the balcony of the royal palace now seem a distant memory, although a small number of

Real Monasterio de la Encarnación

MAP PAGE 38, POCKET MAP A10
Plaza de la Encarnación 1 Tours only
(some in English) Tues–Sat 10am–2pm
& 4–6.30pm, Sun & holidays 10am–3pm.
Charge; joint ticket with Monasterio
de las Descalzas Reales available.
Ⓦ patrimonionacional.es. Ⓜ Ópera.
Founded in 1611 by Felipe III and
his wife Margarita de Austria, this
convent was intended as a retreat
for titled women and merits a visit
for its reliquary alone – one of the
most important in the Catholic
world. The solemn granite facade
is the hallmark of architect Juan
Gómez de Mora, also responsible
for the Plaza Mayor. Much of
the painting contained within is
uninspiring, but there are some
interesting items, including an
extensive collection of royal
portraits and a highly prized
collection of sculptures of Christ.
The library-like **reliquary** contains
more than 1500 saintly relics
from around the world: skulls,
arms encased in beautifully ornate
hand-shaped containers and bones
from every conceivable part of the
body. The most famous of the lot
is a small glass bulb said to contain
the blood of St Pantaleón – a
fourth-century doctor martyr –
which supposedly liquefies at
midnight every July 26 (the eve
of his feast day). Great tragedies
are supposed to occur if the blood
fails to liquefy. The tour ends
with a visit to the Baroque-style
church which features a beautifully
frescoed ceiling and a marble-
columned altarpiece.

Monasterio de las Descalzas Reales

MAP PAGE 38, POCKET MAP C10–C11
Plaza de las Descalzas 3. Tours
only (some in English): Tues–Sat
10am–2pm & 4–6.30pm, Sun & hols
10am–3pm. Charge; joint ticket with
Convento de la Encarnación available.
Ⓦ patrimonionacional.es. Ⓜ Callao, Sol
or Ópera.

One of the less well-known treasures
of Madrid, the "Monastery of
the Barefoot Royal Ladies" was
originally the site of a medieval
palace. The building was
transformed by Juana de Austria
into a convent in 1564, and the
architect of El Escorial, Juan
Bautista de Toledo, was entrusted
with its design. Juana was the
youngest daughter of the Emperor
Charles V and, at the age of 19,
already the widow of Prince Don
Juan of Portugal. Royal approval
meant that it soon became home
to a succession of titled ladies
who brought with them an array
of artistic treasures, helping the
convent accumulate a fabulous
collection of paintings, sculptures
and tapestries. The place is still
unbelievably opulent and remains
in use as a religious institution,
housing 23 shoeless nuns of the
Franciscan order.

The magnificent main staircase
connects a two-levelled cloister,
lined with small but richly
embellished chapels, while the
Tapestry Room contains an
outstanding collection of early
seventeenth-century Flemish
tapestries based on designs by
Rubens. The other highlight of
the tour is the Joyería (Treasury),
piled high with jewels and relics
of uncertain provenance. Royal
portraits and beautiful, wooden
sculptures, most of unknown
origin, decorate other rooms.

San Ginés

MAP PAGE 38, POCKET MAP C11
C/Arenal 13. Mon–Sat 8.45am–1pm &
6–8.45pm, Sun 9.45am–1.45pm & 5.45–
8.45pm. Free. Ⓦ parroquiadesangines.es
Ⓜ Ópera or Sol.
Of Mozarabic origin (built by
Christians under Moorish rule),
this ancient church was completely
reconstructed in the seventeenth
century. There is an El Greco canvas
of the moneychangers being chased
from the temple in the Capilla del
Cristo (on show Mon 12.30pm).

Shops

Discos La Metralleta

MAP PAGE 38, POCKET MAP C10

Plaza San Martín 1°-B
Ⓦ discoslametralleta.com. Mon–Sat
10am–2.30am & 4.30–9pm. Ⓜ Ópera.

Hidden away in a shopping gallery of
an underground carpark you can pick
up some bargain flamenco, Spanish
pop or mainstream rock on vinyl
or CD at this iconic second-hand
record shop that was once a stall at
the Rastro. If you can't find what you
want try *La Gramola*, another record
store just a short walk up the hill at
C/Postigo San Martín 4.

La Melguiza

MAP PAGE 38, POCKET MAP B12

C/Santiago 12 Ⓦ lamelguiza.es. Ⓜ Ópera.

Delightful little shop selling products
made from *azafrán* (saffron) from
La Mancha. Apart from buying the
spice itself, there is a range of soaps
and shampoos and gourmet products
such as white chocolate flavoured
with cardamon and saffron or
pomegranate and saffron marmalade.

Cafés

Café de Oriente

MAP PAGE 38, POCKET MAP A11

Plaza de Oriente 2 Ⓦ cafedeoriente.es. Ⓜ Ópera.

Elegant but pricey Parisian-style
café with a popular *terraza* looking
across the plaza to the palace. The
café was opened in the 1980s by a
priest, Padre Lezama, who ploughs
his profits into various charitable
schemes. There's an equally smart
bar, *La Botillería* next door. €

Chocolatería San Ginés

MAP PAGE 38, POCKET MAP C12

Pasadizo de San Ginés 11
Ⓦ chocolateriasangines.com. Ⓜ Sol or Ópera.

A Madrid institution, this café,
established in 1894, serves *chocolate con
churros* (thick hot chocolate with deep-
fried hoops of batter) to perfection
– just the thing to finish off a night

of excess. It's an almost compulsory
madrileño custom to end up here after
the clubs close, before heading home
for a shower and then off to work. €

Restaurants

La Bola

MAP PAGE 38, POCKET MAP A10

C/Bola 5 Ⓦ labola.es. Ⓜ Santo Domingo
or Ópera.

Opened back in 1870, *La Bola*
is renowned for its lunchtime
cocido madrileño (soup followed by
chickpeas and a selection of meats),
cooked in the traditional way over
a wood fire. Don't plan on doing
anything energetic afterwards.
Service can be a little brusque. €€

El Buey

MAP PAGE 38, POCKET MAP C4

Plaza de la Marina Española 1
Ⓦ restauranteelbuey.com. Ⓜ Santo
Domingo or Ópera.

A meat-eaters' paradise, specializing in
superb steak that you fry yourself on
a hotplate. Great side dishes include
a mouth-watering leek and seafood
slice, plus home-made desserts, with a
highly drinkable house red. €€

Casa Gallega

MAP PAGE 38, POCKET MAP B12, C11

C/Bordadores 11 Ⓦ lacasagallega.com.
Ⓜ Ópera or Sol.

An airy and welcoming *marisquería*
that has been importing seafood
on overnight trains from Galicia
since opening in 1915. Costs vary
according to the market price of the
fish or shellfish that you order. *Pulpo*
(octopus) and *pimientos de Padrón*
(small peppers, spiced up by the
odd fiery one) are brilliantly done
and relatively inexpensive. €€€

Entre Suspiro y Suspiro

MAP PAGE 38, POCKET MAP B10

C/Caños de Peral 3
Ⓦ entresuspiroysuspiro.com. Ⓜ Ópera.

Given Madrid's links with Latin
America, this is one of surprisingly
few good Mexican restaurants in the

city. Quesadillas, tacos and some imaginative takes on traditional dishes are served up in pleasant surroundings, although it is rather cramped. €€

El Escarpín

MAP PAGE 38, POCKET MAP C11
C/Hileras 17 ⓦ elescarpinsidreria.com.
ⓜ Ópera.

Asturian bar-restaurant offering quality regional specialities including *chorizo a la sidra* (chorizo with cider), *fabes con almejas* (beans with clams), an appetite-satisfying *cachopo* (two veal fillets sandwiching a ham-and-cheese filling and coated in breadcrumbs). Eat tapas at the bar or try the brick-lined dining room. €€€€

Gloria Bendita

MAP PAGE 38, POCKET MAP B12
C/Santiago 3 ⓦ bit.ly/GloriaBenditaMadrid.
ⓜ Ópera.

Friendly, brick-lined restaurant with a small outdoor terrace at the quieter end of this street, offering a very tasty selection of meat, fish and vegetarian dishes, and plenty of options to share. The red prawn, coconut milk and coriander croquetas are excellent, as are the artichokes in *cabrales* sauce. €€

Tapas Bar

Arbonaida Bar

MAP PAGE 38, POCKET MAP A12
C/Santiago 11 ⓣ 639 500 068. ⓜ Ópera.
Small, friendly bar serving up a range of imaginatively presented home-made Andalucian tapas dishes including *salmorejo* (a thick tomato soup), *flamenquín* (fried pork and cheese rolls) and tuna. €

Bar

El Anciano Rey de los Vinos

MAP PAGE 38, POCKET MAP C6
C/Bailén 19 ⓦ elancianoreydelosvinos.es.
ⓜ Ópera.
Traditional bar close to the Palacio Real whose layout, furniture and

decorative tiles have changed little since its foundation back in 1909. Well-poured beer, *vermút*, a decent selection of wine and some good tapas add further to the appeal.

Club

Joy Madrid

MAP PAGE 38, POCKET MAP C11
C/Arenal 11 ⓦ joy-eslava.com. ⓜ Sol or Ópera.

This long-standing club is one of the staples of the Madrid night scene. It has a busy schedule of sessions, catering for everything from reggaeton to seventies disco plus occasional live acts. If you arrive early, there are discounts on the entry fee.

Music venues

La Coquette

MAP PAGE 38, POCKET MAP C11
C/Hileras 14 ⓦ bit.ly/LaCoquetteBar. ⓜ Ópera.
A small, crowded and friendly basement jazz and blues bar. Live acts perform Tuesday–Saturday, and a jam session on Sunday. Closed August.

Chocolate con churros

Rastro, Lavapiés and Embajadores

Lavapiés and Embajadores were originally tough, working-class districts built to accommodate the huge population growth of Madrid in the eighteenth and nineteenth centuries. Traditional sights are thin on the ground, but some original tenement blocks survive and the area is now famous for the Rastro street market. These barrios are also home to the castizos – authentic madrileños – who can be seen decked out in traditional costume during local festivals. The character of these areas has changed, however, in recent years. Young Spaniards and large numbers of immigrants have arrived, meaning that Lavapiés and Embajadores are now Madrid's most racially mixed barrios, with teahouses, curry houses, kebab joints and textile shops sitting alongside some of the most original bars and restaurants in the city. Petty crime can be a problem round here, but the reality is not as dramatic as newspapers suggest.

Iglesia Colegiata de San Isidro

Iglesia Colegiata de San Isidro

MAP PAGE 46, POCKET MAP C14
C/Toledo 37. Daily 7.30am–2pm & 5–9pm (summer 7.30am–1pm & 7–9pm). Tours second Sat in each month 9.30 & 10.15am. Ⓜ Tirso de Molina or La Latina.

Built from 1622 to 1633, this enormous twin-towered church was originally the centre of the Jesuit Order in Spain. After Carlos III fell out with the Order in 1767, he redesigned the interior and dedicated it to the city's patron, San Isidro. Isidro's remains – and those of his equally saintly wife – were brought here in 1769 from the nearby **Iglesia de San Andrés** (see page 31). The church was the city's cathedral from 1886 until 1993 when the **Catedral de la Almudena** (see page 37) was completed. It has a single nave with ornate lateral chapels and an impressive altarpiece.

Mercado del Rastro

Mercado del Rastro

MAP PAGE 46, POCKET MAP D8
Ⓜ La Latina.

Every Sunday morning, the heaving mass of El Rastro flea market takes over Calle Ribera de Curtidores. On offer is just about anything you might need – or more likely might not – from old clothes and military surplus to caged birds and fine antiques. Real bargains are rare, but the atmosphere is enjoyable and the nearby bars are as good as any in the city. Petty theft can be a problem, so keep a close eye on your belongings. If you're looking for something more upmarket, try the antiques shops in **Galerías Piquer** at C/Ribera de Curtidores 29, which are also open Sunday mornings.

La Corrala

MAP PAGE 46, POCKET MAP E8
C/Tribulete 12 & C/Mesón de Paredes
Ⓜ Lavapiés.

Built in 1872 and restored in the 1980s, this is one of many traditional *corrales* (tenement blocks) in Lavapiés, with balconied apartments opening onto a central patio. Plays, especially farces and *zarzuelas* (a mix of classical opera and music hall), used to be performed regularly in *corrales*.

San Cayetano

MAP PAGE 46, POCKET MAP E8
C/Embajadores 15. Variable hours, usually Mon–Sat 9.30am–noon & 6–8pm, Sun 9.30am–2pm. Ⓜ Tirso de Molina or La Latina.

José de Churriguera and Pedro de Ribera, both renowned for their extravagant designs, were involved in the design of the elaborate facade, which dates from 1761. Most of the rest of the church was destroyed in the Civil War and has since been rebuilt.

Plaza Lavapiés

MAP PAGE 46, POCKET MAP F8
Ⓜ Lavapiés.

In the Middle Ages, bustling Plaza Lavapiés was the core of Jewish Madrid, with the synagogue situated on the site now occupied by the Teatro Valle-Inclán. Today, with its Chinese, Arabic and African inhabitants, it remains a cosmopolitan place, and the

Cine Doré

plaza, along with Calle Argumosa running off from its southeastern corner, is an animated spot, with a variety of bars and cafés.

Calle Atocha

MAP PAGE 46, POCKET MAP E6–H8
Ⓜ Estación del Arte or Antón Martín.
Calle Atocha, one of the old ceremonial routes from Plaza Mayor to the basilica at Atocha, forms the northeastern border of Lavapiés. At its southern end it's a mishmash of fast-food and touristy restaurants, developing, as you move north up the hill, into a strange mixture of cheap hostels, fading shops, bars, lottery kiosks and sex emporia. With its brash neon lighting and shiny black facade, the huge sex shop at no. 80, stands unashamedly opposite a convent and the site of an old printing house that produced the first edition of the first part of Miguel de Cervantes' epic novel *Don Quixote*.

Cine Doré

MAP PAGE 46, POCKET MAP F14
C/Santa Isabel 3 Ⓦ entradasfilmoteca. gob.es. Ⓜ Antón Martín.

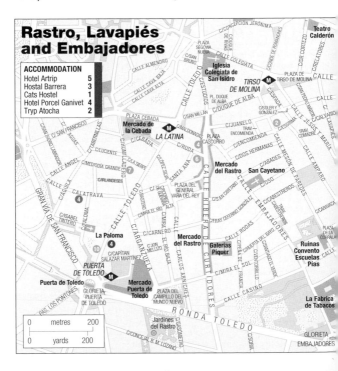

At the end of the narrow Pasaje Doré alley is the Cine Doré, the **oldest cinema** in Madrid. Dating from 1922 with a later Modernista/Art Nouveau facade, it's now the **Filmoteca Nacional**, an art-house cinema with bargain prices and a pleasant, inexpensive café/restaurant.

La Casa Encendida

MAP PAGE 46, POCKET MAP F9
Ronda Valencia 2 Tues–Sun 10am–10pm. Charge for some exhibitions. Ⓦ lacasaencendida.es. Ⓜ Embajadores.
At the southern end of Lavapiés is La Casa Encendida, an alternative cultural centre with an internationalist and slightly avant-garde streak. Hosting everything from groundbreaking art exhibitions and concerts to films and workshops, the centre has an open and welcoming atmosphere, a decent café and is worth investigating if you happen to be in the area.

Museo del Ferrocarril

MAP PAGE 46, POCKET MAP H9
Paseo de las Delicias 61. June–Sept daily 10am–3pm; Oct–May Mon–Fri 9.30am–3pm, Sat & holidays 10am–7pm, Sun 10am–3pm. Charge. Ⓦ museodelferrocarril.org. Ⓜ Delicias.
The Museo del Ferrocarril (Railway Museum) is one of the largest historic railroad collections in Europe and contains an impressive assortment of engines, carriages and wagons that once graced the train lines of Spain. The museum, which is housed in the handsome old station of Delicias, also has a fascinating collection of **model railways** and an atmospheric little café in one of the more elegant carriages. On Saturdays from Oct to June you can ride on the miniature railway in the garden area at the back.

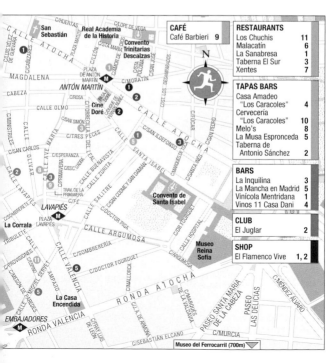

CAFÉ	
Café Barbieri	9

RESTAURANTS	
Los Chuchis	11
Malacatín	6
La Sanabresa	1
Taberna El Sur	3
Xentes	7

TAPAS BARS	
Casa Amadeo "Los Caracoles"	4
Cervecería "Los Caracoles"	10
Melo's	8
La Musa Espronceda	5
Taberna de Antonio Sánchez	2

BARS	
La Inquilina	3
La Mancha en Madrid	5
Vinícola Mentridana	1
Vinos 11 Casa Dani	4

CLUB	
El Juglar	2

SHOP	
El Flamenco Vive	1, 2

Shop

El Flamenco Vive

MAP PAGE 46, POCKET MAP G7
C/Duque de Fernán Núñez 5
Ⓦ elflamencovive.com. Ⓜ Antón Martín.
A fascinating little slice of Andalucía
in Madrid, specializing in all things
flamenco, from dresses to shoes and
earrings. Musical instruments and
CDs can be found in a sister shop at
nearby C/Moratín 6.

Café

Café Barbieri

MAP PAGE 46, POCKET MAP F8
C/Ave María 45 Ⓦ cafebarbieri.es. Ⓜ lavapiés.
A relaxed fin de siècle bar-café-
restaurant, with mirrors, marble
tables, a wide selection of coffees,
vermút on tap, Italian food and
occasional live music. €

Restaurants

Los Chuchis

MAP PAGE 46, POCKET MAP F8
C/Amparo 82 Ⓦ facebook.com/
LosChuchisBar. Ⓜ Lavapiés.
Run by Brit Scott Preston, this little
gastro bar is a welcoming place serving
some great food. The *menú del día* is
great value and features options such
as hake with pesto, shepherd's pie and
a selection of tasty soups. €

Malacatín

MAP PAGE 46, POCKET MAP D8
C/Ruda 5 Ⓦ malacatin.com. Ⓜ La Latina.
Established in 1895 to serve wine to
local workmen, this authentic *castizo*
restaurant serves generous helpings
of arguably the best *cocido* (stew) in
the city for a reasonable price. You
can also sample it at the bar. Closed
mid-July to mid-August. €€

La Sanabresa

MAP PAGE 46, POCKET MAP G14
C/Amor de Diós 12. ☎ 914 290 338.
Ⓜ Antón Martín.
Unpretentious and popular local
comedor with reasonably priced
dishes. There is a *menú* available
for both lunch and in the evening
with lots of home-made options
such as *fabada*, fried asparagus and
artichokes. Don't miss the battered
aubergines. Closed August. €

Taberna El Sur

MAP PAGE 46, POCKET MAP F7
C/Torrecilla del Leal 12. Ⓦ facebook.com/
Elsurdetorrecilla. Ⓜ Antón Martín.
Friendly bar/restaurant with an
interesting array of good-value
raciones including *ropa vieja*
(Cuban-style beef), *salmorejo*,
moussaka and vegetarian
hamburgers. A good wine selection
and a welcoming atmosphere. €

Xentes

MAP PAGE 46, POCKET MAP C8
C/Humilladero 13 Ⓦ xentes.es. Ⓜ La Latina
or Puerta de Toledo.
Deservedly popular Galician
restaurant with a wide-ranging
menu, including excellent *arroz
caldoso* (rice dish) accompanied by
a range of seafood ingredients, plus
a two-person *menú degustación* and
a tasty selection of steaks. €€

Tapas bars

Casa Amadeo "Los Caracoles"

MAP PAGE 46, POCKET MAP D7
Plaza Cascorro 18 Ⓦ caracolesdeamadeo.com.
Ⓜ La Latina.
A favourite since the 1940s and the
founder Amadeo is still in charge,
offering *madrileño* speciality tapas
from the eponymous *caracoles*
(snails) to *callos*, *oreja* and *rabo de
toro*. It's heaving on Sundays when
the Rastro is in full swing. €

Cervecería "Los Caracoles"

MAP PAGE 46, POCKET MAP C8
C/Toledo 106 Ⓦ bit.ly/LosCaracolesMadrid.
Ⓜ Puerta de Toledo.
Rough-and-ready standing-room-
only bar dating back to the 1920s,

which specializes in snails, washed down with local *vermút del grifo* (draught vermouth). Closed July. €

Melo's

MAP PAGE 46, POCKET MAP F8
C/Ave María 44 Ⓜ Lavapiés.

Standing room only at this very popular Galician bar serving *zapatillas* (huge toasted sandwiches filled with *lacón* – shoulder of pork – and cheese) plus delicious *pimientos de padrón* (hot-fried green peppers). Closed August. €

La Musa Espronceda

MAP PAGE 46, POCKET MAP G7
C/Santa Isabel 17 Ⓦ bit.ly/LaMusa Espronceda. Ⓜ Estación del Arte or Antón Martín.

Great-value tapas – classics such as *tortilla* and *croquetas* and creative bites such as fried aubergine with honey – served in this friendly retro Lavapiés local. €

Taberna de Antonio Sánchez

MAP PAGE 46, POCKET MAP E7
C/Mesón de Paredes 13 Ⓦ tabernaantonio sanchez.com. Ⓜ Tirso de Molina.

Said to be Madrid's oldest *taberna*, this seventeenth-century bar has a stuffed bull's head (in honour of the founder' son, who was killed by one) and a wooden interior. Lots of *finos*, plus *jamón* tapas or *tortilla de san isidro* (salt cod omelette). €

Bars

La Inquilina

MAP PAGE 46, POCKET MAP F8
C/Ave María 39 Ⓦ tabernalainquilina.com. Ⓜ Lavapiés.

This deceptively large, bohemian bar hosts regular art exhibitions and acoustic concerts. It serves an interesting range of artisan beers, vermouth, and Portuguese and French tapas. €

La Mancha en Madrid

MAP PAGE 46, POCKET MAP F9
C/Miguel Servet 13 ☎ 910 617 213.

Vermouth with a slice

Ⓜ Lavapiés.

Friendly, old-style bar with a small outdoor terrace. A great place for a beer or glass of wine accompanied by some very good cheese, *chorizo* and *salchichón* (cured sausage). €

Vinícola Mentridana

MAP PAGE 46, POCKET MAP G7
C/San Eugenio 9 ☎ 912 65 93 82. Ⓜ Antón Martín.

Atmospheric traditional wine bar lined with dusty old bottles, a favourite with the Lavapiés crowd. A great selection of wine and beer, plus appetising canapés and tapas. Closed August. €

Vinos 11 Casa Dani

MAP PAGE 46, POCKET MAP B13
C/Calatrava 11 ☎ 913 652 621. Ⓜ La Latina.

Long-standing, atmospheric, *castizo* bar serving up a great *vermút* and a simple, but appetising menu of tapas at very reasonable prices. €

Club

El Juglar

MAP PAGE 46, POCKET MAP F8
C/Lavapiés 37 Ⓦ salajuglar.com. Ⓜ Lavapiés.

Down-to-earth club with DJs playing funk and soul. Also hosts regular live concerts.

Sol, Santa Ana and Huertas

The busy streets around Puerta del Sol, Plaza Santa Ana and Huertas are the bustling heart of Madrid and the reference point for most visitors to the capital. The city began to expand here during the sixteenth century and the area subsequently became known as Barrio de las Letras (literary neighbourhood) because of the many authors and playwrights – including Cervantes – who made it their home. Today, the literary theme continues, with theatres, bookshops and cafés proliferating alongside the Círculo de Bellas Artes (Fine Arts Institute), the Teatro Español (historic theatre specializing in classic works) and the Congreso de Los Diputados (Parliament). For art lovers, there's the Real Academia de Bellas Artes de San Fernando museum, but for most visitors the main attraction is the vast array of traditional bars, particularly concentrated around the picturesque Plaza Santa Ana.

Puerta del Sol

MAP PAGE 52, POCKET MAP D11
Ⓜ Sol.

This half-moon-shaped plaza, thronged with people at almost any hour of the day, marks the epicentre of Madrid and, indeed,

of Spain – **Kilometre Zero**, an inconspicuous stone slab on the south side of the square, is the spot from which all distances in the country are measured. Opposite is an equestrian bronze of King Carlos III, and to the east a statue

Casa de Correos, Puerta del Sol

of Madrid's emblem, *el oso y el madroño* (bear and strawberry tree).

The square has been a popular meeting place since the mid-sixteenth century, when it was the site of one of the main gates into the city. Its most important building is the Casa de Correos, built in 1766 and originally the city's post office. Under Franco it became the headquarters of the much-feared security police and it now houses the main offices of the Madrid regional government. The Neoclassical facade is crowned by the nation's most famous clock which officially ushers in the New Year: on December 31, *madrileños* pack Puerta del Sol and attempt to scoff twelve grapes – one on each of the chimes of midnight – to bring themselves good luck for the next twelve months.

The square has also witnessed several incidents of national importance, including the slaughter of a rioting crowd by Napoleon's marshal, Murat, aided by the infamous Egyptian cavalry, on May 2, 1808. The massacre is depicted in Goya's canvas, *Dos de Mayo*, now hanging in the Prado (see page 64).

Plaza Santa Ana

MAP PAGE 52, POCKET MAP F13
Ⓜ Sol or Antón Martín.

The main reason for visiting vibrant Plaza Santa Ana is the mass of bars, restaurants and cafés on the square itself and in the nearby streets that bring the area alive in the evenings.

The square was one of a series created by Joseph Bonaparte, whose passion for open spaces led to a remarkable remodelling of Madrid in the six short years of his reign. It's dominated by two distinguished buildings at either end: to the west, the *ME Madrid Reina Victoria*, a giant white confection of a hotel; to the east, the nineteenth-century Neoclassical Teatro Español. There has been a playhouse on this site since 1583, and the current theatre is the oldest in Madrid, its facade decorated with busts of famous Spanish playwrights.

Tiled facade, Santa Ana

Casa Museo Lope de Vega

MAP PAGE 52, POCKET MAP G13
C/Cervantes 11. Tues–Sun 10am–6pm.
Closed mid-July to mid-Aug. Access only with guided tours (in English; every 30 mins; 45 mins), which must be booked in advance, see website. Free.
Ⓦ casamuseolopedevega.org. Ⓜ Antón Martín.

Situated in the heart of the Huertas district, the reconstructed home of the great Golden Age Spanish dramatist offers a fascinating glimpse of life in seventeenth-century Madrid. Lope de Vega, a prolific writer with a tangled private life, lived here for 25 years until his death in 1635 at the age of 72. The house itself has been furnished in authentic fashion using the inventory left at the writer's death and highlights include a chapel containing some of his relics, his study with a selection of contemporary books, an Arabic-style drawing room and a delightful courtyard garden.

Cervantes lived and died at no. 2 on the same street and though the original building has long gone, a plaque above a shop marks the site.

Sol, Santa Ana and Huertas

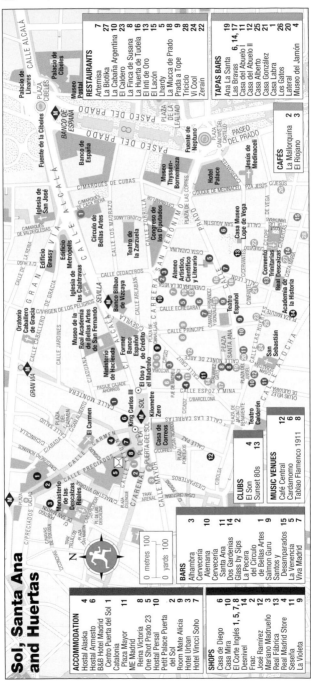

ACCOMMODATION

Hostal Alaska	4
Hostal Armesto	6
B&B Hotel Madrid	1
Centro Puerta del Sol	1
Catalonia	
Plaza Mayor	11
ME Madrid	
Reina Victoria	8
One Shot Prado 23	5
Hostal Persal	10
Petit Palace Puerta	
del Sol	2
Room Mate Alicia	9
Hotel Urban	3
Hotel Vincci Soho	7

SHOPS

Casa de Diego	6
Casa Mira	10
El Corte Inglés	1, 5, 7, 8
Desnivel	14
Fnac	2
José Ramírez	12
Mariano Madrueño	4
Real Fábrica	13
Real Madrid Store	3
Seseña	11
La Violeta	9

BARS

Alhambra	3
Cervecería	
Alemana	11
Santa Ana	14
Dos Gardenias	2
Glass by Sips	
La Pecera	
del Círculo	
de Bellas Artes	1
Salmon Guru	9
Santos y	
Desamparados	15
La Venencia	5
Viva Madrid	7

CLUBS

El Son	4
Sunset 80s	13

MUSIC VENUES

Café Central	12
Cardamomo	6
Tablao Flamenco 1911	8

RESTAURANTS

Artemisa	7
La Biotika	27
La Cabaña Argentina	10
El Caldero	23
La Finca de Susana	8
La Huerta de Tudela	16
El Inti de Oro	13
El Lacón	15
Lhardy	5
La Mucca de Prado	18
Prada a Tope	9
Triciclo	28
Vi Cool	24
Zerain	22

TAPAS BARS

Ana La Santa	19
Las Bravas	6, 14, 17
Casa del Abuelo I	11
Casa del Abuelo II	12
Casa Alberto	25
Casa González	21
Casa Labra	1
Los Gatos	26
Lateral	20
Museo del Jamón	4

CAFÉS

La Mallorquina	2
El Riojano	3

Plaza de Cibeles

Ateneo Artístico, Científico y Literario

MAP PAGE 52, POCKET MAP G12
C/Prado 2 Ⓦ ateneodemadrid.com.
Ⓜ Antón Martín or Sevilla.

The Ateneo (literary, scientific and political club) was founded after the 1820 Revolution and provided a focus for the new liberal political ideas circulating at that time. The exterior is neo-Plateresque in style, while the inside features a Neoclassical lecture theatre, the study of Manuel Azaña (President of the Second Republic during the Civil War) and a splendid reading room. It also has a café, restaurant and hosts occasional exhibitions.

Congreso de los Diputados

MAP PAGE 52, POCKET MAP G12
Plaza de las Cortes. Guided tours Fri noon, Sat 10.30am, 11.15am & noon; plus of the exhibition on Monday noon; reserve through the website, bring a passport. Closed Aug & holidays. Free. Ⓦ congreso.es. Ⓜ Sevilla.

The lower house of the **Spanish parliament** meets in a rather unprepossessing nineteenth-century building; its most distinguished feature is the two bronze lions that guard the entrance, made from a melted-down cannon captured during the African War of 1859–60. Sessions can be visited by appointment only. It is also possible to book for a tour of an exhibition in the basement beneath the Congreso on Monday at noon. This takes in several important rooms and the chamber with the bullet holes left by mad Colonel Tejero and his Guardia Civil associates in the abortive coup of 1981.

Calle Alcalá

MAP PAGE 52, POCKET MAP E11–J10
Ⓜ Sol or Sevilla.

An imposing catalogue of Spanish architecture lines Calle Alcalá, an ancient thoroughfare that originally led to the university town of Alcalá de Henares. It starts at Puerta del Sol; in this first stretch, look out particularly for the splendid early twentieth-century wedge-shaped building, which was once the Banco Espanol de Crédito, but has now been gutted to make way for a luxury hotel and shopping mall. The Banco de Bilbao Vizcaya, with its Neoclassical facade complete with charioteers on top, and the Baroque Ministerio de Hacienda (Inland Revenue) are similarly impressive.

Iglesia de San José

MAP PAGE 52, POCKET MAP G10
C/Alcalá 41 Mon–Fri 7am–12.30pm & 6.30–8.30pm, Sat 9.30am–12.30pm, Sun 9.30am–12.30pm & 6.30–8.30pm. Ⓜ Banco de España.

The red-brick Iglesia de San José, near the junction with Gran Vía, dates back to the 1730s and was the last building designed by the prolific Pedro de Ribera. The interior holds the ornate Santa Teresa de Ávila chapel and an impressive collection of colourful images of Christ and the Virgin Mary.

Iglesia de las Calatravas

MAP PAGE 52, POCKET MAP F11
C/Alcalá 25. Mon 7.45am–1pm, Tues–Fri 7.45am–1pm & 6–8pm, Sat 6.30–8pm, Sun 11.30am–1pm. Ⓦ iglesiacalatravas.com. Ⓜ Sevilla.

The pastel-pink Baroque Iglesia de las Calatravas was built in the seventeenth century for the nuns of the Calatrava, one of the four Spanish military orders. Inside, it contains a fantastically elaborate gold altarpiece by José Churriguera.

Museo de la Real Academia de Bellas Artes de San Fernando

MAP PAGE 52, POCKET MAP F11
C/Alcalá 13 Tues–Sun 10am–3pm, Closed Aug. Charge, free Wed. Ⓦ realacademia bellasartessanfernando.com. Ⓜ Sevilla.

Established by Felipe V in 1744 and housed in its present location since 1773, the Museo de la Real Academia de Bellas Artes de San Fernando is one of the most important art galleries in Spain. Its reorganized displays some interesting French and Italian work and an extraordinary collection of Spanish paintings, including El Greco, Velázquez, Murillo, Tàpies and Picasso.

The Goya section has two revealing self-portraits, several depictions of the despised royal favourite *Don Manuel Godoy*, the desolate representation of *The Madhouse* and *The Burial of the Sardine* (a popular procession that continues to this day in Madrid).

The gallery also holds the national copper engraving collection, which includes Goya etchings and several

Museo de la Real Academia de Bellas Artes de San Fernando

of the copper plates used for his *Capricho* series on show in the Prado.

Círculo de Bellas Artes

MAP PAGE 52, POCKET MAP G11
C/Marqués de Casa Riera 2. Exhibitions Tues–Sun 11am–2pm & 5–9pm. Charge. Ⓦ circulobellasartes.com. Ⓜ Banco de España.

This striking 1920s Art Deco building, crowned by a statue of Pallas Athene, is home to one of Madrid's best arts centres. Inside, there's a theatre, music hall, galleries, cinema, café (see page 62) and spectacular roof-top bar (charge for entry). For many years a stronghold of Spain's intelligentsia, it attracts the city's arts and media crowd, but is not exclusive, nor expensive. As the Círculo is theoretically a members-only club, it issues day membership on the door.

Plaza de Cibeles

MAP PAGE 52, POCKET MAP J10
Ⓜ Banco de España.

Encircled by four of the most monumental buildings in Madrid, Plaza de Cibeles is one of the city's most famous landmarks. At its centre, and marooned in a sea of never-ending traffic, is the late eighteenth-century fountain and statue of the goddess Cybele riding in a lion-drawn chariot. Built to celebrate the city's first public water supply, today the fountain is the post-victory congregation point for Real Madrid fans (Atlético supporters bathe in the fountain of Neptune just down the road).

Palacio de Cibeles

MAP PAGE 52, POCKET MAP J10
Exhibitions Tues–Sun 10am–8pm. Ⓦ centrocentro.org. Ⓜ Banco de España.

This grandiose wedding-cake of a building on the eastern side of Paseo del Prado, constructed between 1904 and 1917 by the prolific architect partnership of Antonio Palacios and Joaquín Otamendi, was once Madrid's main post office, but has recently been usurped by the Madrid City

Círculo de Bellas Artes

Council. It is now home to a smart exhibition space, a observation gallery (charge), a café, an expensive restaurant run by Toledan restaurateur Adolfo Muñoz, and an overpriced and rather *pijo* terrace bar, which does offer some great views over the Paseo del Prado.

Palacio de Linares

MAP PAGE 52, POCKET MAP J10
Plaza de Cibeles 2. Exhibitions usually Mon–Sat 11am–8pm, Sun 11am–3pm; guided tours Fri 6pm & 7.30pm, Sat & Sun 11am, noon, 1pm (reservations have to be made in person). Charge. Ⓦ casamerica.es. Ⓜ Banco de España.

This palatial eighteenth-century mansion, built by the Marqués de Linares, is now home to the Casa de América, a cultural organization that promotes Latin American art through concerts, films and exhibitions. At weekends, there are guided tours through the sumptuous mansion decorated with some marvellous frescoes, crystal chandeliers and elaborate tapestries from the Real Fábrica (see page 73). The *palacio* also has an expensive designer restaurant and an excellent summer garden terrace.

Shops

Casa de Diego

MAP PAGE 52, POCKET MAP E11
Puerta del Sol 12. Ⓦ casadediego.info.
Ⓜ Sol.
Old-time shop with helpful staff
selling a fabulous array of Spanish
fans (*abanicos*) ranging from
cheap offerings up to beautifully
hand-crafted works of art costing
as much as €1500. Sells umbrellas,
walking sticks and shawls too.

Casa Mira

MAP PAGE 52, POCKET MAP F12
C/San Jerónimo 30. Ⓦ casamira.es.
Ⓜ Sevilla.
The place to go for *turrón* (flavoured
nougat, eaten by Spaniards at
Christmas) and marzipan. This
family business has been open for
over 150 years since the founder,
Luis Mira, arrived from Asturias and
set up a stall in Puerta del Sol. Closed
July and August.

El Corte Inglés

MAP PAGE 52, POCKET MAP D10 & D11
C/del Carmen. Ⓦ elcorteingles.com. Ⓜ Sol
or Callao.

The Spanish department store *par
excellence*. It's not cheap, but the
quality is very good, the staff are
highly professional (the majority
speak English) and there's a
gourmet section on the ninth floor
of the Callao branch with fantastic
views over the city (see page 87).

Desnivel

MAP PAGE 52, POCKET MAP F14
Plaza Matute 6 Ⓦ libreriadesnivel.com.
Ⓜ Antón Martín.
A great selection of maps and
guides if you fancy a hike in the
nearby Sierra Guadarrama.

Fnac

MAP PAGE 52, POCKET MAP D10
C/Preciados 28 Ⓦ fnac.es. Ⓜ Callao.
Department store with sections for
books, videos, music and electrical
equipment. Also sells concert
tickets.

José Ramírez

MAP PAGE 52, POCKET MAP D12
C/Paz 8 Ⓦ guitarrasramirez.com. Ⓜ Sol.
The Ramírez family have been
making handcrafted guitars since
1882 and, even if you are not
a budding flamenco artist, this

Real Madrid Store

beautiful old shop is still worth a visit to appreciate these works of art used by some of the world's leading musicians.

Mariano Madrueño

MAP PAGE 52, POCKET MAP C10
C/Postigo San Martín 6
Ⓦ marianomadrueno.es. Ⓜ Callao.
Traditional wine seller's, established in 1895, where there's an overpowering smell of grapes as you peruse its vintage-crammed shelves. Intriguing tipples include potent Licor de Hierbas from Galicia and home-made Pacharán (aniseed liqueur with sloe berries).

Real Fábrica

MAP PAGE 52, POCKET MAP G13
C/Cervantes 9 Ⓦ realfabrica.com.
Ⓜ Antón Martín.
Stocking a range of historic Spanish brands from food and drink to home decor and gifts, this beautifully laid-out shop is a great place to pick up an original souvenir.

Real Madrid Store

MAP PAGE 52, POCKET MAP D11
C/Carmen 3 Ⓜ Sol.
Club store where you can pick up replica shirts and all manner of – very expensive – souvenirs related to the club's history. There is another branch at Real's Bernabéu stadium (see page 94).

Seseña

MAP PAGE 52, POCKET MAP E12
C/Cruz 23 Ⓦ sesena.com. Ⓜ Sol.
Open since 1901, this elegant shop specializes in traditional *madrileño* capes for royalty and celebrities. Clients have included Luis Buñuel, Gary Cooper and Hillary Clinton.

La Violeta

MAP PAGE 52, POCKET MAP F12
Plaza de Canalejas 6 Ⓦ lavioletaonline.es.
Ⓜ Sol or Sevilla.
Old-style confectionary store founded in 1915 and famous for its *violetas*, delicate sweets made from the essence of the violet flower.

Cakes on display at La Mallorquina

They also sell violet marmalade, honey and tea as well as more traditional delights for the sweet-toothed. Closed August.

Cafés

La Mallorquina

MAP PAGE 52, POCKET MAP D12
Puerta del Sol 8
Ⓦ pastelerialamallorquina.es. Ⓜ Sol.
Historic Madrid café, ideal for breakfast or sweet snacks. The shop is downstairs, but try one of their *napolitanas* (cream slices) in the upstairs salon that overlooks Puerta del Sol. €

El Riojano

MAP PAGE 52, POCKET MAP D12
C/Mayor 10 Ⓦ pasteleriaelriojano.com.
Ⓜ Sol.
Traditional patisserie shop founded back in 1855 and café selling a wonderful range of Spanish-style sweets and cakes, such as *buñuelos de viento* (balls of chocolate, custard or cream covered in batter) and *torrijas* (bread cooked in milk, egg, sugar, cinnamon and lemon). Closed August. €

Restaurants

Artemisa

MAP PAGE 52, POCKET MAP F12

C/Ventura de la Vega 4 ⓦ restaurantes vegetarianosartemisa.com. Ⓜ Sevilla.

Established vegetarian and vegan restaurant, with a long gluten-free menu including excellent *croquetas*, tacos and moussaka. There is a good-value set lunch too. €€

La Biotika

MAP PAGE 52, POCKET MAP G14

C/Amor de Dios 3 ⓦ labiotika.es. Ⓜ Antón Martín.

This ground-breaking eco restaurant and shop has been on the scene for decades. It offers vegetarian, vegan and macrobiotic menus which change on a daily basis and special options for people with food allergies and intolerances. €

La Cabaña Argentina

MAP PAGE 52, POCKET MAP F12

C/Ventura de la Vega 10 ⓦ lacabanaargentina.es. Ⓜ Sevilla.

El Riojano

One of the best Argentine eateries in the city. Excellent-quality meat with all the best Argentine cuts (*el bife de lomo alto* is a house favourite) and classic desserts including *panqueques*. There are pasta dishes and fish options too at this friendly place. €€

El Caldero

MAP PAGE 52, POCKET MAP F13

C/Huertas 15 ⓦ elcaldero.com. Ⓜ Antón Martín.

Murcian restaurant specialising in rice dishes, in particular *arroz al caldero* which was originally a humble dish made by the region's fishermen. *El Caldero* prides itself on maintaining the traditional method of preparation and using the best ingredients. The salads and starters include fried aubergines and a tomato and salted cod salad. €€

La Finca de Susana

MAP PAGE 52, POCKET MAP F12

C/Princípe 10 ⓦ bit.ly/LaFincaSusana. Ⓜ Sevilla.

One of a chain of good-value restaurants set up by a group of Catalan friends (another, *La Gloria de Montera*, is just off Gran Vía, while a third, *Ginger*, is near Plaza Santa Ana). Food isn't out of this world and service is a bit impersonal, but it does a series of set menus at a decent price. €€

La Huerta de Tudela

MAP PAGE 52, POCKET MAP G13

C/Prado 15 ⓦ lahuertadetudela.com. Ⓜ Sevilla.

With wonderful fresh produce from the region of Navarra as the central attraction, this eatery has earned a well-deserved reputation for high quality seasonal dishes such as oyster mushroom risotto, roast pepper and, haricot beans and cod stew. There is a special taster menu and one for vegetarians, vegans and coeliacs too. €€€

El Inti de Oro

MAP PAGE 52, POCKET MAP F12
C/Ventura de la Vega 12 ⓦ intideoro.es.
Ⓜ Antón Martín.

The friendly staff at this good-
value Peruvian restaurant are
more than ready to provide
suggestions for those new to the
cuisine. The *ceviche clásico* (raw
fish marinated in lime juice) is a
wonderful dish; the pisco sour,
a cocktail of Peruvian liquor,
lemon juice, egg white and sugar
is also recommended; while for
newcomers there is a taster menu.
(Also at C/Amor de Dios.) €€

El Lacón

MAP PAGE 52, POCKET MAP F12
C/Manuel Fernández y González 8
ⓦ mesonellacon.com. Ⓜ Sol.

An old-style Spanish *meson* tucked
away in a small street close to Plaza
Santa Ana, with plenty of seats
upstairs. Great *pulpo, caldo gallego*
(meat and vegetable broth) and
empanadas. They also do a very
decent *menú del día* and *tablas* of
fish, meat, charcuterie or vegetables
for sharing. Closed August. €

Lhardy

MAP PAGE 52, POCKET MAP E12
C/San Jerónimo 8 ⓦ lhardy.com. Ⓜ Sol.

Once the haunt of royalty, this is
one of Madrid's most beautiful
and famous restaurants. It's greatly
overpriced – expect to pay well over
€70 per head for a three-course meal
– but on the ground floor, there's a
wonderful bar/shop where you can
have breakfast or snack on canapés,
fino and consommé, without breaking
the bank. Closed August. €€€€

La Mucca de Prado

MAP PAGE 52, POCKET MAP F13
C/Prado 16 ⓦ bit.ly/LaMucca. Ⓜ Antón
Martín or Sevilla.

Easy-going, good-value restaurant
with a combination of Spanish and
international dishes, including pasta,
pizzas, burgers and fish. There is an
imaginative and varied weekday set
lunch at a decent price too. €

La Violeta

Prada a Tope

MAP PAGE 52, POCKET MAP F12
C/Príncipe 11 ⓦ pradaatopemadrid.com.
Ⓜ Sol.

Produce from the El Bierzo region
of León at this popular chain of
restaurants. The *morcilla* (black
pudding), *empanada de Cacabelos*
(a sort of pasty with chorizo, potato
and onion) and *tortilla* are extremely
tasty, while the smooth house wines
provide the ideal accompaniment. €

Triciclo

MAP PAGE 52, POCKET MAP G14
C/Santa María 28 ⓦ restaurantetriciclo.
com. Ⓜ Antón Martín.

Originally set up by a trio of young
chefs in 2013 with the aim of
creating a restaurant where they
themselves would like to eat. The
results are impressive and *Triciclo*
serves up a wide range of innovative
dishes, such as prawn with shiso and
mango, or oxtail cannelloni with
mushroom sauce, but it comes at a
price. If you can't book a table, try
the more informal sister restaurant
Tandem (ⓦ ilgirointandem.com).
at No 39 in the same street, which
specializes in Italian cuisine with a
modern touch. €€€

SOL, SANTA ANA AND HUERTAS

Vi Cool

MAP PAGE 52, POCKET MAP F13
C/Huertas 12 Ⓦ vi-cool.com.
Ⓜ Antón Martín.

Originally established by Catalan celebrity chef Sergi Arola as a more affordable outlet for his renowned food, the low-key, minimalist interior is the setting for some simple but classy and creative offerings including meat and spinach cannelloni, fried langoustines in a curry and mint sauce, and gourmet hamburgers and pizzas. There are tapas menus and a reasonably priced weekday set lunch. €€

Zeraín

MAP PAGE 52, POCKET MAP G13
C/Quevedo 3 Ⓦ bit.ly/ZerainMadrid.
Ⓜ Antón Martín.

Basque cider house serving excellent meat and fish dishes. The *chuletón* (T-bone steak) is the speciality, but it also does a very good *tortilla de bacalao* and grilled *rape* (monkfish). There are a range of set menus, including one for vegetarians and one for under-12s. Closed August. €€€

Ana La Santa

Tapas bars

Ana La Santa

MAP PAGE 52, POCKET MAP E13
Plaza Santa Ana 14 Ⓦ bit.ly/AnaLaSantaME.
Ⓜ Sol or Antón Martín.

A stylish bar/restaurant housed in smart surroundings in the lobby of the *ME Madrid Reina Victoria* hotel at one end of Plaza Santa Ana. On offer is a mixture of classic *raciones* with a modern touch: Thai-style mussels; sun-dried tomato, aubergine and parmesan *croquetas*; or mushrooms and cashew nuts are the sort of tempting dishes on the menu. €€

Las Bravas

MAP PAGE 52, POCKET MAP E12 & E13
C/Alvarez Gato 3 Ⓦ lasbravas.com. Ⓜ Sol.
Standing room only at these two bars, where, as the name suggests, *patatas bravas* and *tortilla con salsa bravas* are the thing – they patented their own version of the spicy sauce. The other branch is at Pasaje Mathéu 5. €

Casa del Abuelo I

MAP PAGE 52, POCKET MAP E12
C/Victoria 12 Ⓦ lacasadelabuelo.es. Ⓜ Sol.
A tiny, atmospheric bar serving just their own cloyingly sweet red wine (stick with a beer instead) and delicious prawns – try them *al ajillo* (in garlic) or *a la plancha* (grilled) – which are cooked up in the tiny corner kitchen. €

Casa del Abuelo II

MAP PAGE 52, POCKET MAP E12
C/Núñez de Arce 5 Ⓦ lacasadelabuelo.es.
Ⓜ Sol.
There's a *comedor* (dining room) at the back of this classic Madrid bar, with a selection of traditional *raciones* – the *croquetas* and *gambas* are great – to wash down with some of the house wine. €

Casa Alberto

MAP PAGE 52, POCKET MAP F13
C/Huertas 18 Ⓦ casaalberto.es.
Ⓜ Antón Martín.

Traditional *tasca* that has resisted the passage of time since it was founded back in 1827. Good *caracoles* (snails), *gambas* (prawns) and great *croquetas*, ideally accompanied by a glass of house vermouth. €

Casa González

MAP PAGE 52, POCKET MAP F13
C/León 12 ⓦ casagonzalez.es. Ⓜ Antón Martín.
Friendly delicatessen/tapas bar with an extensive range of wines and cheese and serving up some great tapas including a fantastic *ajoarriero* (cod in garlic and pine nuts), speciality sausage from around Spain, and some imaginative *tostas* covered in a variety of patés. €

Casa Labra

MAP PAGE 52, POCKET MAP D11
C/Tetuán 12 ⓦ casalabra.es. Ⓜ Sol.
Dating from 1869 – and where the Spanish Socialist Party was founded ten years later – this traditional and highly popular place retains much of its original interior. Order a drink at the bar and a *ración* of *bacalao* (salted cod fried in batter) or some of the best *croquetas* in town. There's also a restaurant at the back serving classic *madrileño* food. Be prepared to queue. Closed August. €

Los Gatos

MAP PAGE 52, POCKET MAP H13
C/Jesús 2 ⓦ cervecerialosgatos.com.
Ⓜ Antón Martín.
Decorated with a multifarious collection of curiosities including a model of a choirboy with sunglasses, a jazz musician and a horned gramophone, this old-style bar serves up an excellent selection of canapés, *raciones* and beer for its loyal clientele. €

Museo del Jamón

MAP PAGE 52, POCKET MAP E12
C/San Jerónimo 6 Ⓜ Sol
ⓦ museodeljamon.com.
This is the largest branch of this unpretentious Madrid chain, from whose ceilings are suspended hundreds of *jamones* (hams). The best – and they're not cheap – are

Museo del Jamón,

the *jabugos* from the Sierra Morena, though a *racion* of *jamón serrano* will only cost you a few euros. €

Bars

Alhambra

MAP PAGE 52, POCKET MAP E12
C/Victoria 9 ☏ 915 210 708. Ⓜ Sol.
Friendly tapas bar by day, fun disco bar by night, with the crowds spilling over into the neighbouring *El Buscón* bar.

Cervecería Alemana

MAP PAGE 52, POCKET MAP F13
Plaza de Santa Ana 6
ⓦ cerveceriaalemana.com. Ⓜ Sol or Antón Martín,
Traditional old beer house, dating back to 1904, and once frequented by Hemingway. Order a *caña* (draught beer) and go easy on the tapas, as the bill can mount up fast. Closed August.

Cervecería Santa Ana

MAP PAGE 52, POCKET MAP F13
Plaza de Santa Ana 10 ⓦ cerveceria santaana.com. Ⓜ Sol or Antón Martín.
Has tables outside on the plaza, and offers a wide selection of

62

beers, friendly service and a good selection of tapas. Always packed at night.

Dos Gardenias

MAP PAGE 52, POCKET MAP G14
C/Santa María 13 ⓦ facebook.com/dosgardenias.madrid. Ⓜ Antón Martín.
Intimate and relaxed little bar in the Huertas area where you can chill out in their comfy chairs, sip on a mojito, and escape from the hubbub of the city outside.

Glass by Sips

MAP PAGE 52, POCKET MAP F12
C/San Jerónimo 34 ⓦ hotelurban.com.
Ⓜ Sevilla.
Housed in the ultra-chic *Hotel Urban* (see page 130), this glamorous cocktail bar offers an extensive menu of wines, sherries, vermút and gins as well as its own original cocktails and bitesize tapas.

La Pecera del Círculo de Bellas Artes

MAP PAGE 52, POCKET MAP G11
C/Alcalá 42 ⓦ lapeceradelcirculo.com.
Ⓜ Banco de España.
Stylish bar in this classy arts centre, complete with reclining nude

Casa Labra

sculpture, chandeliers and sofas, and a pleasant lack of pretensions. Service can be slow though. Also serves up breakfasts and a set lunch.

Salmon Guru

MAP PAGE 52, POCKET MAP F13
C/Echegaray 21 ⓦ salmonguru.es.
Ⓜ Sevilla or Antón Martín.
Excellent cocktails in this fun gastro-bar run in a characterful street to the east of Plaza Santa Ana. Mirrors, neon lights and comic book heroes adorn the walls, while behind the bar the innovative cocktail menu includes the vodka, Campari, Cointreau and red fruit "La Vie En Rose", and the tequila-based combination "Mad Bunny", well as a selection of non-alcoholic mocktails. There is a small selection of tapas on offer too.

Santos y Desamparados

MAP PAGE 52, POCKET MAP G14
Costanilla Desamparados 4 ⓦ bit.ly/SantosDesamparados. Ⓜ Antón Martín.
Attentive, friendly service in this atmospheric little cocktail bar offering an extensive list of classics and original mixes accompanied by a menu of "finger food". Popular before and after dinner.

La Venencia

MAP PAGE 52, POCKET MAP F12
C/Echegaray 7 Ⓦ lavenencia.com.
Ⓜ Sevilla.

Dilapidated, atmospheric, wood-
panelled bar that's great for sherry
sampling. The whole range is here,
served from wooden barrels, and
accompanied by delicious olives
and *mojama* (dry salted tuna).
Closed August.

Viva Madrid

MAP PAGE 52, POCKET MAP F12
C/Manuel Fernández y González 7
Ⓦ vivamadrid1856.com. Ⓜ Antón Martín
or Sevilla.

This fabulous tiled bar and longtime
stalwart of the Madrid night scene
has been converted into a cocktail
bar under the guidance of Diego
Cabrera, but still retains its old
charm. A great selection of *vermút*
and classic cocktails served up with
a select range of creative tapas.

Clubs

El Son

MAP PAGE 52, POCKET MAP E12
C/Victoria 6 Ⓦ facebook.com/
DiscotecaElSon. Ⓜ Sol.

Latin rhythms and dancing at this
popular *discoteca* close to Sol. Salsa,
merengue. Bachata and reggaeton are
the order of the day. There are expert
dancers who will show you some of
the moves too. Cover charge.

Sunset 80s

MAP PAGE 52, POCKET MAP G13
C/Huertas 31 Ⓦ muyretro.com. Ⓜ Antón Martín.
Good atmosphere at this small,
but friendly retro disco-bar playing
Spanish and international music from
the 60s, 70s and 80s. Cover charge.

Music venues

Café Central

MAP PAGE 52, POCKET MAP E13
Plaza del Ángel 10 Ⓦ cafecentralmadrid.
com. Ⓜ Tirso de Molina.

Tablao Flamenco 1911

Small, renowned jazz club that
gets the odd big name, plus strong
local talent (charge for gigs). The
Art Deco café which serves up a
lunchtime set menu and cocktails is
worth a visit in its own right.

Cardamomo

MAP PAGE 52, POCKET MAP F12
C/Echegaray 15 Ⓦ cardamomo.com.
Ⓜ Antón Martín or Sevilla.

This flamenco bar has evolved
into a respected fully blown *tablao*,
with shows lasting about an hour
– prices vary, and include a drink.
Check the website for the schedule.

Tablao Flamenco 1911

MAP PAGE 52, POCKET MAP E13
Plaza Santa Ana 15 Ⓦ tablaoflamenco1911.
com. Ⓜ Sevilla or Antón Martín.

One of the prime reasons to visit this
flamenco *tablao* is the stupendous
painted tiles that adorn the facade
and the Mudéjar decor within which
once featured in Almodóvar's 1991
classic *Tacones Lejanos* (High Heels).
This new club in the former premises
of *Villa Rosa* now puts on three
enjoyable, tourist-oriented shows a
night, with a range of ticket options,
including tapas.

Paseo del Arte and Retiro

Madrid's three world-class art galleries are all located within a kilometre of each other along what is known as the Paseo del Arte. The Prado, the most renowned of the three, houses an unequalled display of Spanish art, an outstanding Flemish collection and some impressive Italian work. The Thyssen-Bornemisza, based on one of the world's greatest private art collections, provides a dazzling excursion through Western art from the fourteenth to the late twentieth century. Finally, the Centro de Arte Reina Sofía displays contemporary art, including Picasso's iconic masterpiece Guernica. The area around the Paseo del Prado has two beautiful green spaces: the Jardines Botánicos and the Parque del Retiro, as well as lesser-known sights including the fascinating Real Fábrica de Tapices (Royal Tapestry Workshop) and the Museo Naval. It isn't an area renowned for its bars, restaurants and nightlife, but there are plenty of decent places for a drink or lunch.

Museo del Prado

MAP PAGE 66, POCKET MAP J13–14
Mon–Sat 10am–8pm, Sun & hols 10am–7pm. Charge, free Mon–Sat 6–8pm, Sun & hols 5–7pm, for under-18s and students. Ⓦ museodelprado.es. Ⓜ Estación del Arte or Banco de España.

The Prado is Madrid's premier tourist attraction and one of the oldest and greatest collections of art in the world, largely amassed by the Spanish royal family over the last two hundred years.

Reproducing a painting in the Museo del Prado

Tickets are purchased at the Puerta de Goya opposite the *Hotel Ritz* on C/Felipe IV and the entrance is round the back at the Puerta de los Jerónimos, which leads into the museum extension. To avoid the large ticket queues, buy them from the museum website. Audio guides (extra charge) are available at the entrance.

The museum, which was given a new lease of life following the addition of the controversial €152 million Rafael Moneo-designed extension, is set out according to national schools. To follow the route proposed by the museum, bear right upon entering and head into the central hallway, the Sala de las Musas; from here you are guided through the collections on the ground floor before being directed upstairs.

The coverage of Spanish paintings begins with some striking twelfth-century Romanesque frescoes. Beyond is a stunning anthology that includes just about every significant Spanish painter, from the adopted Cretan-born artist El Greco (Domenikos Theotokopoulos), who worked in Toledo in the 1570s, to Francisco de Goya, the outstanding painter of eighteenth-century Bourbon Spain. Don't miss the breathtaking collection of work by Diego Velázquez, including his masterpiece, *Las Meninas* (room 12).

No visit is complete without taking in Goya's deeply evocative works, *Dos de Mayo* and *Tres de Mayo* (room 64), and his disturbing series of murals known as the *Pinturas Negras* (*Black Paintings*; room 67) with their mix of witches, fights to the death and child-eating gods. The artist's remarkable versatility is clear when these are compared with his voluptuous portraits of the *Maja Vestida* (*Clothed Belle*) and *Maja Desnuda* (*Naked Belle*; room 38).

Statue of Velázquez, Museo del Prado

The Italian paintings include the most complete collection by painters from the Venice School in any single museum, among them Titian's magnificent equestrian portrait, *Emperor Carlos V at Mühlberg* (room 27). There are also major works by Raphael and epic masterpieces from Tintoretto, Veronese and Caravaggio.

The early Flemish works are even more impressive and contain one of Hieronymus Bosch's greatest triptychs, the hallucinogenic *Garden of Earthly Delights* (room 56A). Look out, too, for the works of Pieter Bruegel the Elder, whose *Triumph of Death* must be one of the most frightening canvases ever painted, Rogier van der Weyden's magnificent *Descent from the Cross* (room 58) and the extensive Rubens collection.

German and French painting is less well represented but still worth seeking out – especially the pieces by Dürer, Cranach and Poussin – while on the second floor (Room 79B) is a glittering display of the jewels that belonged to the Grand Dauphin Louis, son of Louis XIV

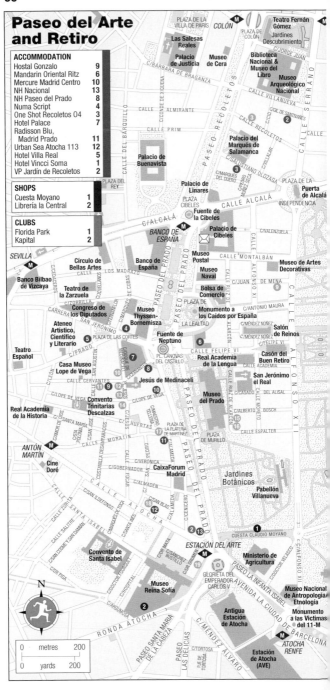

Paseo del Arte and Retiro

ACCOMMODATION
Hostal Gonzalo	9
Mandarin Oriental Ritz	6
Mercure Madrid Centro	10
NH Nacional	13
NH Paseo del Prado	8
Numa Script	4
One Shot Recoletos 04	3
Hotel Palace	7
Radisson Blu, Madrid Prado	11
Urban Sea Atocha 113	12
Hotel Villa Real	5
Hotel Vincci Soma	1
VP Jardín de Recoletos	2

SHOPS
Cuesta Moyano	1
Librería la Central	2

CLUBS
Florida Park	1
Kapital	2

CAFÉS

Café el Botánico	16
Murillo Café	15

RESTAURANTS

El Barril de las Letras	11
Bodega de los Secretos	18
El Buey	1
La Castela	5
La Catapa	7
La Montería	4
Al Mounia	3
Saraiba	2
Taberna Laredo	6
Taberna Pedraza	8
Viridiana	9

TAPAS BARS

El Brillante	19
Cervecería Cervantes	12
Dis Tinto Taberna	10
La Fábrica	14
La Platería	17
La Taberna de Dolores	13

and father of Felipe V, Spain's first Bourbon king.

The new wing houses temporary exhibition spaces, restoration workshops and a sculpture gallery as well as a restaurant, café and shops.

Museo Reina Sofía

MAP PAGE 66, POCKET MAP G8
Mon & Wed–Sat 10am–9pm, Sun 10am–2.30pm. Charge, free Mon & Wed–Sat 7–9pm, Sun after 12.30pm, and for under-18s, students and over-65s. Ⓦ museoreinasofia.es. Ⓜ Estación del Arte.

An essential stop on the Madrid art circuit is the Museo Reina Sofía, an immense exhibition space providing a permanent home for the Spanish collection of modern and contemporary art, including the Miró and Picasso legacies.

If the queues at the main entrance are too long, try the alternative one in the extension on the Ronda de Atocha.

As well as its collection of twentieth-century art, the museum has a theatre, cinema, excellent bookshops, a print, music and photographic library, a restaurant, bar and café in the basement and a peaceful inner courtyard garden. A guidebook examining some of the key works is available from the shops. At the entrance, there are audio guides in English (charge), which provide informative commentaries for the first-time visitor.

The **permanent collection** has been reorganised into "episodes" spanning the second and fourth floors of the museum. Episode one "avant-garde territories" begins on the second floor with a section examining the origins of modern Spanish art, largely through the artistic nuclei that developed in Barcelona, Madrid and Paris at the end of the nineteenth century. The collection ranges across the original Sabatini building and Jean Nouvel's

Guernica

Superbly displayed and no longer protected by the bulletproof glass and steel girders that once imprisoned it, Picasso's *Guernica* is a monumental icon of twentieth-century Spanish art and politics which, despite its familiarity, still has the ability to shock. Picasso painted it in response to the bombing of the Basque town of Gernika in April 1937 by the German Luftwaffe, acting in concert with Franco, during the Spanish Civil War. In the preliminary studies, displayed around the room, you can see how he developed its symbols – the dying horse, the woman mourning, the bull and so on – and then return to the painting to marvel at how he made it all work. Picasso determined that the work be "loaned" to the Museum of Modern Art in New York while Franco remained in power, meaning that the artist never lived to see it displayed in his home country – it only returned to Spain in 1981, eight years after Picasso's death and six after the demise of Franco.

If you plan to visit all three art museums on the Paseo del Prado during your stay, it's well worth buying the **Paseo del Arte ticket**, which is valid for a year and allows one visit to each museum at a substantial saving, although it does not include the temporary exhibitions. It's available at any of the three museums. The Paseo del Arte Essential app provides an explanation of 24 of the leading works to be found in the museums.

Brushstroke, by Roy Lichtenstein, at the Museo Reina Sofía

79 million-euro state-of-the-art extension, which is built around an open courtyard topped by a striking delta-shaped, metallic, crimson-coloured roof.

Midway round the second floor is the Reina Sofía's main draw – Picasso's *Guernica* (see box, page 68), an emblematic piece that has always evoked strong reactions. Strong sections on Cubism – in the first of which Picasso is again well represented – and the Paris School follow. Dalí and Miró make heavyweight contributions too in the Surrealism section. The development of Dalí's work and his variety of techniques are clearly displayed, with pieces ranging from the classic *Muchacha en la Ventana* to famous Surrealist works such as *El Enigma de Hitler*. Impressive works from the Cubist Juan Gris are intermingled with a fascinating collection of Spanish sculpture to complete the circuit on this floor.

The collection continues on the fourth floor, although here it's no match for the attractions of the previous exhibits. This section covers Spain's postwar years and includes Spanish and international examples of abstract and avant-garde movements such as Pop Art, Constructivism and Minimalism, one of the highlights being Francis Bacon's *Figura Tumbada* (*Reclining Figure*). Worth hunting out is the section on photography during the years of Franco's dictatorship, and the work by British artists Henry Moore and Graham Sutherland. There are also some striking pieces by the Basque abstract sculptor Chillida and Catalan Surrealist painter Antoni Tàpies. Other elements of the collection focus on experimental, revolutionary and feminist art, dealing with themes from the final years of the Franco dictatorship to the present day. The museum is also home to temporary exhibition spaces.

Museo Thyssen-Bornemisza

MAP PAGE 66, POCKET MAP H12
Mon noon–4pm, Tues–Sun 10am–7pm.
Charge, permanent collection free Mon.
Ⓦ museothyssen.org. Ⓜ Banco de España.

This fabulous private collection, assembled by Baron Heinrich Thyssen-Bornemisza, his son Hans Heinrich and his former beauty-queen wife Carmen was first displayed here in 1993 and contains pieces by almost every major Western artist since the fourteenth century.

An cleverly intergrated extension, built on the site of an adjoining mansion, gives it room to house temporary exhibitions and Carmen's collection, which is particularly strong on nineteenth-century landscape, North American, Impressionist and Post-Impressionist work.

The Baron's collection begins on the second floor with pre-Renaissance work from the fourteenth century. This is followed by a wonderful array of Renaissance portraits by, among others, Ghirlandaio, Raphael and Holbein, including the latter's commanding *Henry VIII*. Beyond are some equally impressive pieces by Titian, Tintoretto, El Greco, Caravaggio and Canaletto. The second floor ends with a comprehensive collection of portraits, still lifes and landscapes by the Dutch masters.

The first floor continues with some splendid nineteenth-century

Picasso's *Harlequin with a Mirror*, Museo Thyssen-Bornemisza

American landscapes. There are strong contributions from Van Gogh – most notably one of his last and most gorgeous works, *Les Vessenots* – and excellent coverage of the vivid Expressionist work of Kandinsky, Nolde and Kirchner, as well as the apocalyptic *Metropolis* by George Grosz.

The collection continues with some outstanding Cubist work from Picasso, Braque, Gris and Mondrian, brilliantly prefigured by Cezanne's striking *Seated Man* This contrasts beautifully with the the realism and hyper-realism of American artists Edward Hopper and Richard Estes, while Roy Lichtenstein's iconic Pop Art creation *Woman in a Bath*. provides a fitting climax. There are also some marvellous pieces by Miró, Pollock and Chagall. Surrealism is, not surprisingly, represented by Dalí, while the final galleries include some eye-catching work by Bacon, Lichtenstein and Freud.

Carmen's collection on the ground floor is based on a family inheritance not included in the original bequest to the state. Highlights include Jan Brueghel's *Garden of Eden*, four Rodin sculptures, a soothing collection of Impressionist works by Pissarro, Monet, Renoir, Degas and Sisley and an outstanding array of work by Gauguin and the Post-Impressionists.

Parque del Retiro

MAP PAGE 66, POCKET MAP J4–K7
Daily: summer 6am–midnight; winter 6am–10pm. Ⓜ Retiro, Ibiza, Atocha Renfe, Estación del Arte or Banco de España.

The origins of the wonderful Parque del Retiro (Retiro Park) go back to the early seventeenth century when Felipe IV produced a plan for a new palace and French-style gardens, the Buen Retiro. Of the buildings, only the ballroom (Casón del Buen Retiro) and the Hall of Realms (Salón de Reinos) remain.

The park's 330-acre expanse offers the chance to jog, rollerblade, cycle, picnic, row on the lake, have your fortune told, and – above all – **promenade**. The busiest day is Sunday, when half of Madrid turns out for the *paseo*.

Promenading aside, there's almost always something going on in the park, including concerts in the Quiosco de Música, performances by groups of South American pan-piping musicians by the lake and, on summer weekends, puppet shows by the Puerta de Alcalá entrance.

Travelling art exhibitions are frequently housed in the graceful **Palacio de Velázquez** (daily: April–Sept 10am–10pm; Oct & March 10am-7pm, Nov–Feb 10am–6pm; free) and the splendid **Palacio de Cristal** (same hours during exhibitions, but closed when raining; free), while the **Centro Cultural Casa de Vacas** (usually daily 10am–9pm; closed Aug) hosts shows, concerts and plays. Look out, too, for the magnificently ostentatious statue to Alfonso XII by the lake and the Ángel Caído, supposedly the world's only public statue to Lucifer, in the south of the park. The Bosque de los Ausentes, 192 olive trees and cypresses planted by the Paseo de la Chopera in memory of the victims who died in the train bombings at the nearby Atocha station on March 11, 2004, is close by.

Puerta de Alcalá

MAP PAGE 66, POCKET MAP J4
Ⓜ **Retiro or Banco de España.**

The Puerta de Alcalá is one of Madrid's most emblematic landmarks. Built in Neoclassical style in 1769 by Francesco Sabatini to commemorate Carlos III's first twenty years on the throne, it was the biggest city gate in Europe at the time. Once on the site of the city's easternmost boundary, it's now marooned on a small island on the traffic-choked Plaza de la Independencia.

Parque del Retiro

Jardines Botánicos

MAP PAGE 66, POCKET MAP H7
Plaza de Murillo 2. Daily 10am–dusk. Charge, free Tues 10am-1pm and for under-18s
Ⓦ rjb.csic.es. Ⓜ **Estación del Arte.**

The delightful botanical gardens were opened in 1781 by Carlos III. The king's aim was to collect and grow species from all over his Spanish Empire, develop a research centre, and supply medicinal herbs and plants to Madrid's hospitals. Abandoned for much of the last century, they were restored in the 1980s and are now home to some 30,000 species from around the globe. Don't miss the hothouse with its amazing cacti or the bonsai collection of former prime minister Felipe González. Temporary exhibitions take place in the Pabellón Villanueva within the grounds.

CaixaForum Madrid

MAP PAGE 66, POCKET MAP H7
Paseo del Prado 36. Daily 10am–8pm. Charge. Ⓦ caixaforum.org/es/madrid.
Ⓜ **Estación del Arte.**

An innovative exhibition space, opened in 2008 by the Catalan savings bank, which complements the existing attractions on the Paseo del Arte. The centre, which hosts a variety of high-quality art shows and exhibitions, is flanked by an eye-catching **vertical garden** designed by French botanist Patrick Blanc in which some 15,000 plants form an organic carpet extending across the wall. There is a decent art bookshop and a restaurant inside, as well.

Museo de Artes Decorativas

MAP PAGE 66, POCKET MAP J5
C/Montalbán 12. Tues–Sat 9.30am–3pm, Sun 10am–3pm, plus Thurs 5–8pm Sept–June. Charge, free Sat 2–3pm, Sun and Thurs eve. Ⓦ bit.ly/MuseoDeArtes. Ⓜ Banco de España.

The national collection of decorative arts is housed in an elegant nineteenth-century mansion. The highlight is its collection of *azulejos* (tiles) and other ceramics with a magnificent eighteenth-century tiled Valencian kitchen on the top floor. The rest of the exhibits include an interesting but unspectacular collection of furniture, a series of reconstructed rooms and objets d'art from all over Spain.

CaixaForum Madrid's vertical garden

Museo Naval

MAP PAGE 66, POCKET MAP J5
Paseo del Prado 5. Tues–Sun 10am–7pm, Aug 10am–3pm, closed public hols. Free (bring ID; voluntary donation requested) Ⓦ armada.mde.es. Ⓜ Banco de España.

As you might expect, the Naval Museum is strong on models, charts and navigational aids relating to Spanish voyages of discovery. Exhibits include the first map to show the New World, drawn in 1500 by Juan de la Cosa, cannons from the Spanish Armada and part of Cortés' standard used during the conquest of Mexico. The room dedicated to the *Nao San Diego*, sunk during a conflict with the Dutch off the Philippines in 1600, contains fascinating items recovered during the salvage operation in the early 1990s.

San Jerónimo el Real

MAP PAGE 66, POCKET MAP H6
C/Ruiz de Alarcón. Daily: mid-Sept to June 10am–1pm & 5–7.30pm; July to mid-Sept 10am–1pm & 6–8pm. Ⓜ Estación del Arte or Banco de España.

Madrid's high-society church was built on the site of a monastery founded in the early sixteenth century by the Catholic monarchs, Fernando and Isabel. It later became the venue for the swearing-in of the heirs to the throne and setting for many royal marriages and coronations (including the former king, Juan Carlos, in 1975). Despite remodelling and the addition of two Gothic towers, the old form of the church is still visible; but the seventeenth-century cloisters have fallen victim to the Prado extension.

Plaza de la Lealtad (Monumento a los Caídos por España)

MAP PAGE 66, POCKET MAP H6
Ⓜ Banco de España.

This aristocratic plaza contains the **Monument to Spain's Fallen**. Originally a memorial to the *madrileños* who died in the 1808 anti-French rebellion (the urn at the base contains their ashes), it was later changed to commemorate all those who have died fighting for Spain, and an eternal flame now burns here. On one side of the plaza stands the opulent *Ritz Hotel*, work of Charles Mewès, architect of the *Ritz* hotels in Paris and London, while opposite is the Madrid stock exchange.

Estación de Atocha

MAP PAGE 66, POCKET MAP J9
Ⓜ Estación del Arte or Atocha Renfe.

The grand Estación de Atocha is now sadly infamous as the scene of the horrific train bombings that killed 192 people and injured close to two thousand in March 2004. A glass memorial to the victims stands just outside one of the entrances on Paseo de la Infanta Isabel. The tower channels light into an underground chamber (access via the station) lined with an inner membrane on which are written messages of condolence. The old station alongside was revamped in 1992 and is a glorious 1880s glasshouse, resembling a tropical garden. It's a wonderful sight from the walkways above, as a constant spray of water rains down on the jungle of vegetation. At the platforms beyond sit the gleaming high-speed AVE trains.

Museo Nacional de Antropología/Etnología

MAP PAGE 66, POCKET MAP J8
C/Alfonso XII 68. Tues–Sat 9.30am–8pm, Sun 10am–3pm. Charge, free Sat after 2pm & Sun. Ⓦ bit.ly/AnthropMuseum. Ⓜ Estación del Arte or Atocha Renfe.

The National Anthropology and Ethnography Museum was founded by the eccentric Dr Pedro Gonzálcz Velasco to house his private collection. The original, rather macabre mix of mummies, skulls and skeletons has been reviewed and edited out of respect for their descendants, and the

Museo Naval

museum now provides an overview of different cultures and customs of people from across the different continents, particularly those linked to Spanish history.

Real Fábrica de Tapices

MAP PAGE 66, POCKET MAP K9
C/Fuentarrabía 2. Guided tours only, with reservations through the website: Mon–Fri 10am, 11am, noon & 1pm, Sept–June also 4pm and 5pm Tues–Thurs. Charge. Ⓦ realfabricadetapices.com. Ⓜ Atocha Renfe or Menéndez Pelayo.

The Royal Tapestry Workshop makes for a fascinating visit. Founded in 1721 and moved to its present site in the nineteenth century, the factory uses processes and machines unchanged for hundreds of years. The handful of workers that remain can be seen coolly looping handfuls of bobbins around myriad strings and sewing up worn-out masterpieces with exactly matching silk. With progress painfully slow – one worker produces a square metre of tapestry every three and a half months – the astronomical prices soon seem easily understandable.

Bookstalls at Cuesta Moyano

Shops

Cuesta Moyano

MAP PAGE 66, POCKET MAP H8
Cuesta de Claudio Moyano
Ⓦ cuestamoyano.es. Ⓜ Estación del Arte.
A row of little wooden kiosks on
a hill close to the Retiro selling
just about every book you could
think of, from secondhand copies
of Captain Marvel to Cervantes.
Other items include old prints
of Madrid and relics from the
Franco era.

Librería la Central

MAP PAGE 66, POCKET MAP G8
Ronda de Atocha 2. Mon & Wed–Sat
10am–7.45pm, Sun 10am–3pm. Ⓦ bit.ly/
LibreriaCentral. Ⓜ Estación del Arte.
Nestled in the interior courtyard
of the Reina Sofía extension, *La
Central* is the best of the art gallery
bookshops, with an extensive range
of posters, coffee-table art books
and more academic tomes.

Cafés

Café el Botánico

MAP PAGE 66, POCKET MAP H7
C/Ruiz de Alarcón 27
Ⓦ restaurantebotanico.com. Ⓜ Estación
del Arte or Banco de España.
Ideal for a refreshing drink after
visiting the Prado; this well-
established café/bar/restaurant has
a shady terrace in a quiet street
by the botanical gardens. It serves
good beer and a selection of snacks,
though it is over-priced if you want
anything more substantial. €

Murillo Café

MAP PAGE 66, POCKET MAP H7
C/Ruiz de Alarcón 27 Ⓦ murillocafe.com.
Ⓜ Estación del Arte or Banco de España.
Another good bet for a coffee break
if you are in between museum
visits or on your way to the Retiro.
Serves breakfasts, brunch and other
meals too if you cannot keep the
hunger at bay. €€

Restaurants

El Barril de las Letras

MAP PAGE 66, POCKET MAP G13
C/Cervantes 28 Ⓦ barrildelasletras.com.
Ⓜ Antón Martín.

Smart, modern-looking bar-
restaurant specializing in Galician
seafood products so it isn't cheap,
but the *raciones* are delicious, and if
you stick to the bar you can sample
a few dishes rather than going for a
whole meal. The seafood rice dishes
are a very good bet, and better
value if you are on a budget. €€€

Bodega de los Secretos

MAP PAGE 66, POCKET MAP G7
C/San Blas 4 Ⓦ bodegadelossecretos.com.
Ⓜ Estación del Arte.

Located in an atmospheric brick-
lined wine cellar (access is difficult)
just behind the CaixaForum
exhibition space, this restaurant offers
a range of stylishly-presented Spanish
dishes with a modern twist and has
an excellent wine list too. Mains
include duck with apple gnocchi or
mushroom and asparagus risotto. €€€

El Buey

MAP PAGE 66, POCKET MAP K3
C/General Diaz Porlier 9
Ⓦ restauranteelbuey.com. Ⓜ Goya.

Top-quality meat accompanied by
an excellent array of starters, side
dishes and salads in this friendly little
restaurant near the Retiro. Prices are
reasonable considering the quality, and
there is a very good value three-course
set menu with a decent house red. €€

La Castela

MAP PAGE 66, POCKET MAP K4
C/Dr Castelo 22 Ⓦ restaurantelacastela.com.
Ⓜ Ibiza.

Mouthwateringly good *raciones* in
this very popular bar-restaurant in
the up-market area to the east of
the Retiro. The fried fish, *almejas*
(clams) and seafood *croquetas* are
superb. Prices are pretty good for
the quality. Get there early if you
want a seat. €€

La Catapa

MAP PAGE 66, POCKET MAP K4
C/Menorca 14 Ⓦ tabernalacatapa.
eatbu.com. Ⓜ Ibiza.

Very popular bar-restaurant serving
up a varied menu featuring fresh,
in-season ingredients as well as
specialities such as steak tartare,
red curry mussels, fried squid and
excellent home-made tortilla. They
have separate bar and restaurant
menus, but both are delicious. €€

La Montería

MAP PAGE 66, POCKET MAP K4
C/Lope de Rueda 35 Ⓦ lamonteria.es.
Ⓜ Ibiza.

This inconspicuous little restaurant
on the Retiro's eastern edge has
been revamped, and serves some
of the tastiest food in the area.
Excellent fish dishes include hake
and tuna and a mouth-watering
mushroom risotto. The steak and
venison are also very good. €€€

Al Mounia

MAP PAGE 66, POCKET MAP H4
C/Recoletos 5 Ⓦ restaurantealmounia.es.
Ⓜ Banco de España.

Moroccan cooking at its best in the
most established, and atmospheric,

Shellfish tapa

Arabic restaurant in town. The couscous, lamb tagine and desserts are a must. Closed August. €€

Saraiba

MAP PAGE 66, POCKET MAP K4
C/Antonio Acuña 7 Ⓦ restaurantesaraiba.
es. Ⓜ Príncipe de Vergara.

Large Galician restaurant just to the north of the Retiro serving up regional tapas – excellent *pulpo* and *lacón* (shoulder of pork) as you would expect – as well as more substantial dishes such as *arroz meloso con carabineros* (sticky rice with red prawns) and *cochinillo*. €€€

Taberna Laredo

MAP PAGE 66, POCKET MAP K4
C/Dr Castelo 30 Ⓦ tabernalaredo.com.
Ⓜ Ibiza.

Delicious seasonal salads, rice and fish dishes served up with style at this acclaimed bar/restaurant close to the Retiro. Reservations essential. Closed August. €€€

Taberna Pedraza

MAP PAGE 66, POCKET MAP K4
C/Ibiza 38 Ⓦ tabernapedraza.com. Ⓜ Ibiza.

Well-regarded gastro-bar just to the east of the Retiro, run by a married couple, Carmen and Santiago.

Excellent *tortilla* and *croquetas*, as well as a seasonal selection of traditional dishes from around Spain. €€

Viridiana

MAP PAGE 66, POCKET MAP J5
C/Juan de Mena 14 Ⓦ restauranteviridiana.
com. Ⓜ Banco de España.

A bizarre temple of Madrid *nueva cocina* (new cuisine), decorated with photos from Luis Buñuel's film of the same name, and offering mouth-watering creations plus a superb selection of wines. A three-course meal will cost you over €100 a head, but it's an unforgettable experience. Closed Easter and August. €€€€

Tapas bars

El Brillante

MAP PAGE 66, POCKET MAP H8
Glorieta de Emperador Carlos V 8
Ⓦ barelbrillante.es. Ⓜ Estación del Arte.

Down-to-earth, open-all-hours, brightly-lit bar next to the Reina Sofía. Claims to serve the best *calamares bocadillo* (filled baguette) in Madrid, but also does very good *patatas bravas* and *oreja*. Perfect for a quick snack between museum visits. €

Bodega de los Secretos

Cervecería Cervantes

MAP PAGE 66, POCKET MAP H13
Plaza de Jesús 7 ☎ 914 296 093.
Ⓜ Antón Martín or Banco de España.
Great beer and excellent fresh seafood
tapas in this busy little bar just
behind the *Palace Hotel*. The *gambas*
(prawns) go down a treat with a cool
glass of beer, while the *tosta de gambas*
(a sort of prawn toast) is a must. €

Dis tinto Taberna

MAP PAGE 66, POCKET MAP H13
C/Duque de Medinaceli 12 ☎ 917 649 790.
Ⓜ Antón Martín or Banco de España.
Cosy tapas and wine bar offering
a mixture of traditional and more
modern tapas. The *bacalao* and
pulpo tortillas are impressive, while
the *croquetas liquidas* are mouthwateringly good. Follow the wine
recommendations and you can't go
wrong. €

La Fábrica

MAP PAGE 66, POCKET MAP H13
Plaza de Jesús 2 Ⓦ cervezaslafabrica.es.
Ⓜ Antón Martín or Banco de España.
Bustling, friendly bar serving a
delicious range of canapés – the
smoked cod is one of the favourites
– plus chilled beer and good
vermouth. €

La Platería

MAP PAGE 66, POCKET MAP H14
C/Moratín 49 ☎ 914 291 722. Ⓜ Antón
Martín or Estación del Arte.
This bar has a popular summer
terraza geared to a tourist
clientele and a good selection of
reasonably priced tapas available all
day. Service can be a little brusque
though. €

La Taberna de Dolores

MAP PAGE 66, POCKET MAP H13
Plaza de Jesús 4 ☎ 914 292 243.
Ⓜ Antón Martín or Banco de España.
A standing-room-only tiled bar,
decorated with beer bottles from
around the world. The beer is great
and the splendid food specialities
include roquefort and anchovy and
smoked-salmon canapés. €

El Buey restaurant in El Retiro

Clubs

Florida Park

MAP PAGE 66, POCKET MAP K5
Paseo de Panamá Ⓦ floridapark.es.
Ⓜ Ibiza or Príncipe de Vergara.
Iconic multipurpose venue on the
eastern edge of the Retiro, which
has a relaxed, partially outdoor
café/bar known as a La Galería
serving drinks and *raciones*, a
rooftop cocktail bar, an upmarket
and rather pricey restaurant, and a
club with a varied agenda of music
and acts ranging from indie to
flamenco.

Kapital

MAP PAGE 66, POCKET MAP H8
C/Atocha 125 Ⓦ teatrokapital.com.
Ⓜ Estación del Arte.
A seven-floor mega club with an
expensive entry fee, though they do
include two drinks before 1am, and
it caters for practically every taste,
with three dance floors, lasers, go-
go dancers, a cinema and a terraza.
The eclectic musical menu features
disco, house, merengue, salsa, the
ubiquitous reggaeton and even one
floor dedicated to karaoke.

Gran Vía, Chueca and Malasaña

The Gran Vía, one of Madrid's main thoroughfares, effectively divides the old city to the south from the newer parts in the north. Heaving with shoppers and sightseers, it's the commercial heart of the city, and a monument in its own right, with its turn-of-the-twentieth-century, palace-like buildings and offices. North of here, and bursting with bars, restaurants and nightlife, are two of the city's most vibrant barrios: Chueca, focal point of Madrid's gay scene, and Malasaña, former centre of the Movida madrileña, the happening scene of the late 1970s and early 1980s, and still a somewhat alternative area, focusing on lively Plaza Dos de Mayo. As well as the bustling atmosphere, a couple of museums and a number of beautiful churches in the area provide even more reasons for a visit.

Gran Vía

MAP PAGE 80, POCKET MAP D10–G10
Ⓜ Gran Vía.

The Gran Vía (Great Way), built in three stages at the start of the twentieth century, became a symbol of Spain's arrival in the modern world. Financed on the back of an economic boom, experienced as a result of the country's neutrality

in World War I, the Gran Vía is a showcase for a whole gamut of architectural styles, from Modernist to Neo-Rococo.

The finest section is the earliest, constructed between 1910 and 1924 and stretching from C/ Alcalá to the Telefónica skyscraper. Particularly noteworthy are the Edificio Metrópolis (1905–11),

The Edificio Metrópolis on the Gran Vía

complete with cylindrical facade, white stone sculptures, zinc-tiled roof and gold garlands, and the nearby Grassy building (1916–17). The vast 81m-high slab of the Telefónica building was Spain's first skyscraper. During the Civil War it was used as a reference point by Franco's forces to bomb the area. The stretch down to Plaza de Callao is dominated by shops, cafés and cinemas, while the plaza itself is now the gateway to the shoppers' haven of C/Preciados. On the corner is the classic Art Deco Capitol building (1931–33), its curved facade embellished with garish neon signs. Cast your eyes skywards on the final stretch downhill towards Plaza de España to catch sight of an assortment of statues and decorations that top many of the buildings.

Museo Gran Vía 15

MAP PAGE 80, POCKET MAP F10
Gran Vía 15. Daily 11am–9pm. Charge Ⓦ museogranvia15.com. Ⓜ Gran Vía
A new exhibition space with aims to stage experiences showcasing the best of contemporary art. It was inaugurated with an immersive show of Okuda San Miguel's colourful, geometric, surrealist work and promises to stage further eye-catching exhibitions.

Plaza de Chueca

MAP PAGE 80, POCKET MAP G3
Ⓜ Chueca.
The smaller streets north of Gran Vía are home to some of the city's more go-ahead businesses and shops, while in and around Plaza de Chueca, there's a strong neighbourhood feel and a lively gay scene. The area has been rejuvenated in recent years and now holds some enticing streets lined with offbeat restaurants, small private art galleries and unusual corner shops. Calle Almirante has some of the city's most fashionable clothes shops and Calle Augusto Figueroa is the place to go for shoes.

Palacio de Longoria

Las Salesas Reales

MAP PAGE 80, POCKET MAP H3
Plaza de las Salesas. Mon–Fri 9am–1pm & 5–8pm, Sat & Sun 10am–2pm & 6–9pm. Ⓜ Colón.
The Santa Bárbara church was originally part of the convent complex of Las Salesas Reales, founded in 1747. The church is set behind a fine forecourt, while inside, there's a grotto-like chapel, delightful frescoes and stained-glass windows, and some striking green marble altar decoration. The tombs of Fernando VI, his wife Bárbara de Bragança and military hero General O'Donnell lie within.

Sociedad de Autores

MAP PAGE 80, POCKET MAP G3
C/Fernando VI 4 Ⓜ Alonso Martínez.
Home to the Society of Authors, the Palacio de Longoria is the most significant Modernista building in Madrid. Designed in 1902 by the Catalan architect José Grases Riera, its facade features a dripping decoration of flowers, faces and balconies.

Plaza del Dos de Mayo

MAP PAGE 80, POCKET MAP E2
Ⓜ Tribunal or Bilbao.

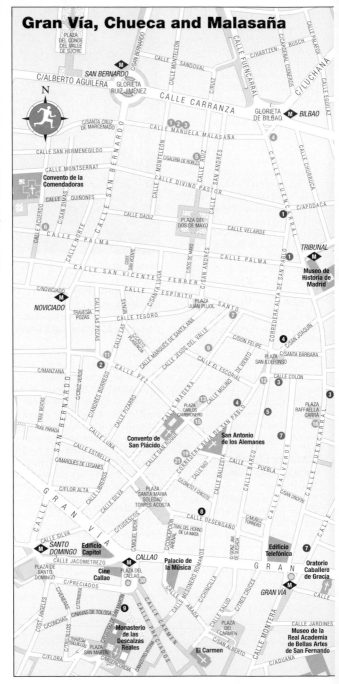

Gran Vía, Chueca and Malasaña

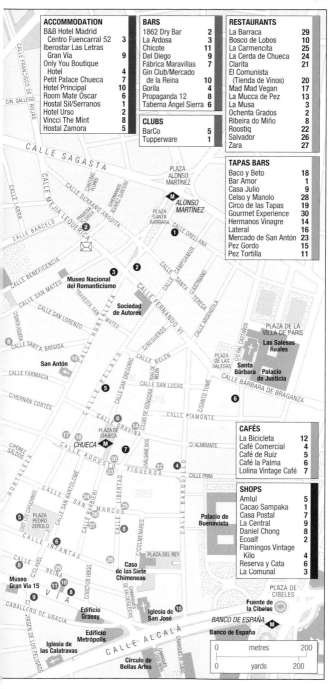

ACCOMMODATION

B&B Hotel Madrid Centro Fuencarral 52	3
Iberostar Las Letras Gran Vía	9
Only You Boutique Hotel	4
Petit Palace Chueca	7
Hotel Principal	10
Room Mate Óscar	6
Hostal Sil/Serranos	1
Hotel Urso	2
Vincci The Mint	8
Hostal Zamora	5

BARS

1862 Dry Bar	2
La Ardosa	3
Chicote	11
Del Diego	9
Fábrica Maravillas	7
Gin Club/Mercado de la Reina	10
Gorila	4
Propaganda 12	8
Taberna Ángel Sierra	6

CLUBS

BarCo	5
Tupperware	1

RESTAURANTS

La Barraca	29
Bosco de Lobos	10
La Carmencita	25
La Cerda de Chueca	24
Clarita	21
El Comunista (Tienda de Vinos)	20
Mad Mad Vegan	17
La Mucca de Pez	13
La Musa	3
Ochenta Grados	2
Ribeira do Miño	8
Roostiq	22
Salvador	26
Zara	27

TAPAS BARS

Baco y Beto	18
Bar Amor	1
Casa Julio	9
Celso y Manolo	28
Circo de las Tapas	19
Gourmet Experience	30
Hermanos Vinagre	14
Lateral	16
Mercado de San Antón	23
Pez Gordo	15
Pez Tortilla	11

CAFÉS

La Bicicleta	12
Café Comercial	4
Café de Ruiz	5
Café la Palma	6
Lolina Vintage Café	7

SHOPS

Amlul	5
Cacao Sampaka	1
Casa Postal	7
La Central	9
Daniel Chong	8
Ecoalf	2
Flamingos Vintage Kilo	4
Reserva y Cata	6
La Comunal	3

Plaza del Dos de Mayo is the centre of a lively bar scene, with people spilling onto the streets that converge on the square. The plaza commemorates the rebellion against occupying French troops in 1808, while the neighbourhood gets its name from a young seamstress, Manuela Malasaña, who became one of the rebellion's heroines.

Museo Nacional del Romanticismo

MAP PAGE 80, POCKET MAP F2
C/San Mateo 13. Tues–Sat 9.30am–8.30pm (Nov–April closes 6.30pm), Sun 10am–3pm. Charge, free Sat after 2pm, Sun, for under-18s and over-65s. Ⓦ bit.ly/RomanticismoMadrid. Ⓜ Tribunal or Alonso Martínez.

The Museo del Romanticismo aims to show the lifestyle and outlook of the late-Romantic era through the recreation of a typical bourgeois residence in the turbulent reign of Isabel II (1833–68), and this it does brilliantly. Overflowing with a marvellously eclectic and often kitsch hoard of memorabilia, the mansion is decorated with some stunning period furniture and ceiling frescoes, together with more

San Antonio de los Alemanes

bizarre exhibits such as the pistol which the satirist Mariano José de Larra used to shoot himself in 1837 after being spurned by his lover.

Museo de Historia de Madrid

MAP PAGE 80, POCKET MAP F2
C/Fuencarral 78. Tues–Sun 10am–8pm (mid-June to mid-Sept closes 7pm). Free. Ⓦ madrid.es/museodehistoria. Ⓜ Tribunal.

Just around the corner from the Museo del Romanticismo, the Museo de Historia de Madrid has been given a new lease of life after a lengthy restoration programme. The former city almshouse was remodelled in the early eighteenth century by Pedro de Ribera and features one of his trademark elaborately decorated Baroque doorways superimposed on a striking red-brick facade. Inside, the museum contains an intriguing collection of paintings, photos, models, sculptures and porcelain, all relating to the history and urban development of Madrid since 1561 (the date it was designated imperial capital by Felipe II). One of the star exhibits is a fascinating 3-D model of the city made in 1830 by military engineer León Gil de Palacio.

San Antonio de los Alemanes

MAP PAGE 80, POCKET MAP E3
Corredera de San Pablo 16. Mon–Sat 10am–2pm & 5–7pm; closed Aug. Charge. Ⓜ Chueca or Callao.

This little church – designed in 1624 by the Jesuit architect Pedro Sánchez and Juan Gómez de Mora for Felipe III – is one of the city's hidden treasures. The elliptical interior is lined with dizzying floor-to-ceiling pastel-coloured frescoes by Neapolitan artist Luca Giordano which depict scenes from the life of St Anthony. The name of the church originates from the fact that Mariana de Austria gifted it to the German catholics who accompanied Maria Ana of Neuberg to the Spanish court when she married the frail Carlos II.

Shops

Amlul
MAP PAGE 80, POCKET MAP G3
C/Pelayo 48 ⓦ shop.amlul.com. ⓜ Chueca.
Set up by Spanish fashion blogger
Gala González, this is the outlet
for her own haute couture lines
of sustainable, ethical women's
clothing produced in Spain. As you
would expect, the skirts, dresses,
tops, jackets and swimwear all
come at a premium price, though
they are designed to last a lifetime.

Cacao Sampaka
MAP PAGE 80, POCKET MAP G3
C/Orellana 4. ⓦ cacaosampaka.com.
ⓜ Alonso Martinez
There's every conceivable shape,
colour and flavour of chocolate
here, ranging from rose and
strawberry to gin and tonic. The
only surprise is that their café menu
has some non-chocolate options.
Closed August.

Casa Postal
MAP PAGE 80, POCKET MAP G3
C/Libertad 37. ⓦ todocoleccion.net.
ⓜ Chueca.
Marvellous old-fashioned shop
for lovers of nostalgia, packed
with postcards, posters, vintage
metal signs and other original
mementos of the city. A good
place for an unconventional
souvenir of Madrid. Closed July
and August.

La Central
MAP PAGE 80, POCKET MAP C10
C/Postigo de San Martín 8 ⓦ lacentral.com.
ⓜ Callao.
Stunning bookshop over four
floors of a beautifully decorated
building just off Plaza Callao. As
well as thumbing through copies
of its comprehensive selection
of Spanish, Latin American and
English classics, you can admire
the frescoed ceilings, check out the
basement cocktail bar or have a
drink in the café.

Mercado de San Antón

Daniel Chong
MAP PAGE 80, POCKET MAP C10
C/Desengaño 22 ⓦ daniel-chong.com.
ⓜ Gran Vía.
Colourful, stylish, eco-friendly
backpacks, handbags, wallets,
laptop cases and other accessories,
all handmade in Spain in
workshops in Lavapiés, Pamplona
and Elche. The staff are friendly
and helpful.

Ecoalf
MAP PAGE 80, POCKET MAP G2
C/Mejía Lequerica, 2 ⓦ ecoalf.com.
ⓜ Alonso Martínez.
High-quality fashion for men and
women, but with a difference;
everything is made from
recycled material. Founded by
Javier Goyeneche in 2012 with the
aim of creating a truly sustainable
business, this sleek-looking store
– which is also fitted out with
recycled materials – is the showcase
for his knitwear, jackets, accessories
and sneakers.

Flamingos Vintage Kilo
MAP PAGE 80, POCKET MAP F3
C/San Joaquín 16 ⓦ bit.ly/FlamingosKilo.
ⓜ Tribunal.
Great selection of quality vintage
clothing, much of which are sold

by weight, in this stylish store with helpful staff close to C/Fuencarral.

Reserva y Cata
MAP PAGE 80, POCKET MAP G3
C/Conde de Xiquena 13
ⓦ reservaycata.com. Ⓜ Chueca.
The very knowledgeable staff at this friendly shop help you select from some of the best new wines in the Iberian peninsula, and run tastings too. There is a wide selection of Spanish liqueurs also available.

La Comunal
MAP PAGE 80, POCKET MAP G2
C/Mejia Lequerica 1 ⓦ lacomunal.es.
Ⓜ Alonso Martínez.
This olive-growers' co-operative outlet has been refurbished and updated, providing all the information you need to help you buy the best olive oils from around Spain. They also organise talks and tastings.

Cafés

La Bicicleta
MAP PAGE 80, POCKET MAP E3
Plaza San Ildefonso 9 ⓦ labicicletacafe.com.
Ⓜ Tribunal.

La Barraca

Café-bar on this little plaza which is a popular hangout for Malasaña hipsters and a good place for breakfast, coffee and evening drinks, though it does get very crowded at weekends. Snacks and small meals are also available too. €

Café Comercial
MAP PAGE 80, POCKET MAP F1
Glorieta de Bilbao 7
ⓦ cafecomercialmadrid.com. Ⓜ Bilbao.
Once in danger of disappearing completely, this Madrid institution has been given a make-over and a new lease of life, though it still has the look and feel of a traditional café with its mirrors and marble tables and remains a great place for a coffee. €

Café de Ruiz
MAP PAGE 80, POCKET MAP E2
C/Ruiz 11 ☏ 663 784 498. Ⓜ Bilbao.
Classic Malasaña café and a great place to while away an afternoon. Discreet background music and good cakes are followed by cocktails and sets by local jazz, swing and folk artists in the evening. €

Café la Palma
MAP PAGE 80, POCKET MAP D2
C/Palma 62 ⓦ cafelapalma.com.
Ⓜ Noviciado.
Part traditional café, part arts and music venue, *Café la Palma* acts as a stage for a myriad of local artists ranging from singer-songwriters to storytellers. It also has popular DJ sessions on many evenings, as well as holding regular open mic nights. Charge for events. €

Lolina Vintage Café
MAP PAGE 80, POCKET MAP E3
C/Espiritu Santo 9 ⓦ lolinacafe.com.
Ⓜ Tribunal.
Step back into the seventies in this friendly retro café in the heart of Malasaña. The decor is on point and the atmosphere relaxed. Serves up breakfasts and lunch as well as cocktails, *vermút*, coffee and cake. €

Restaurants

La Barraca

MAP PAGE 80, POCKET MAP F10

C/Reina 29 🌐 labarraca.es. Ⓜ Bilbao.
Step off the dingy street into this
little piece of Valencia for some of
the best paella in town. The starters –
in particular the *buñuelos de bacalao*
– are excellent, and there's a great
lemon sorbet for dessert too. €€

Bosco de Lobos

MAP PAGE 80, POCKET MAP F3

C/Hortaleza 63 🌐 grupotragaluz.com.
Ⓜ Chueca or Tribunal.
The location is half the attraction
of this delightful Italian restaurant,
tucked away in a garden courtyard
off the main street in the Colegio
de Arquitectos (School of
Architects). On offer are the usual
Italian staples of pizza, pasta and
risottos combined with some more
original starters. There is a *menu del
día* option at lunchtime. €€

La Carmencita

MAP PAGE 80, POCKET MAP G4

C/Libertad 16 🌐 tabernalacarmencita.es.
Ⓜ Chueca.
This traditional *taberna*, whose
roots date back to 1854, reopened
and refurbished in 2013, but
remains faithful to its origins
serving up an authentic range of
classic dishes with carefully sourced
ingredients including traditional
stews, *pollo en pepitoria* (chicken in
an almond sauce), *arroz marinero*
(rice with monkfish) and stuffed
peppers. The carefully selected wine
list contains offerings from some
of Spain's most interesting and
innovative growers. €€€€

La Cerda de Chueca

MAP PAGE 80, POCKET MAP G4

C/Barbieri 15 🌐 lacerdadechueca.es.
Ⓜ Chueca.
Fun, pig-themed, pink decor at this
attentive restaurant in the heart
of Chueca. A short menu offers
speciality pulled-pork hamburgers
with goat's cheese, pork cheek in
red curry sauce, as well as other
options such as marinated salmon
in mango vinaigrette. €€

Clarita

MAP PAGE 80, POCKET MAP E4

Corredera Baja de San Pablo 19
🌐 claritamadrid.es. Ⓜ Callao or Santo
Domingo.
Bar/restaurant in a buzzing street
north of Gran Vía, popular amongst
theatre-goers in the evenings for a
la carte options and set menus, as
well as at lunch, and for breakfasts.
Fusion-style options include
courgette and prawn tempura,
good risottos and a rather expensive
gourmet hamburger. Some
interesting wines on offer too. €€

El Comunista (Tienda de Vinos)

MAP PAGE 80, POCKET MAP G4

C/Augusto Figueroa 35 ☎ 915 217 012.
Ⓜ Chueca.
Step back in time at this long-
established *comedor* that has
changed little since it was given its
unofficial name as a student haunt
under Franco. Home-cooking
at its best; the *sopa de ajo* (garlic
soup) and the *lentejas* (lentils)
are delicious, while *arroz con leche*
and homemade crème caramel are
the favourites for dessert. Closed
mid-August to mid-September. €

Mad Mad Vegan

MAP PAGE 80, POCKET MAP F3

C/Pelayo 19 🌐 madmadvegan.com.
Ⓜ chueca.
A straightforward restaurant with
friendly service and some excellent
vegan burgers, salads and creative
starters. There are plenty of gluten
free options too. €

La Mucca de Pez

MAP PAGE 80, POCKET MAP E3

C/Plaza de Carlos Cambronero 4 🌐 bit.ly/
LaMuccaDePez. Ⓜ Tribunal or Callao.
Popular restaurant with its own
terrace that sits at the top of this
plaza in Malasaña. Food ranges from

Tex-Mex and Italian to Spanish staples like *pimientos de Padrón* and *salmorejo*, though it is the atmosphere that brings most people here. There is a good-value, varied *menu del día* too, but you need to get here early if you want a table. €

La Musa

MAP PAGE 80, POCKET MAP E1
C/Manuela Malasaña 18 ⓦ grupolamusa.com.
Ⓜ Bilbao.

A firm favourite on the Malasaña scene. Very decent-value set lunch, good tapas, generous helpings, a strong wine list and chic decor are all part of *La Musa's* recipe for success – the only real problem is the crowds. Reservations can be made at 1.30pm for lunch and 7 or 8.30pm for evening meals. €

Ochenta Grados

MAP PAGE 80, POCKET MAP E1
C/Manuela Malasaña 10
ⓦ ochentagrados.com. Ⓜ Bilbao.
The idea behind *Ochenta Grados* is to serve traditional main course dishes in miniature, and it works wonderfully. Forget the idea of a starter and a main; just order a few dishes to share from the menu, maybe chilli crab ravioli, duck lasagne or chicken fingers with mustard and honey sauce. €

Ribeira do Miño

MAP PAGE 80, POCKET MAP F3
C/Santa Brígida 1
ⓦ marisqueriaribeiradomino.com.
Ⓜ Tribunal.
Good-value *marisquería*, serving fabulous seafood platters and Galician specialities at great prices; try the slightly more expensive Galician white wine, Albariño. Reservations essential. Closed August. €€

Roostiq

MAP PAGE 80, POCKET MAP G4
C/Augusto Figueroa 47 ⓦ madrid.roostiq. com. Ⓜ Chueca.
Renowned for its *torreznos* (crispy, fried pork belly), Roostiq has its own farm where its chicken and many of the vegetables are sourced and, as you would expect, the quality is top notch. The meat, pizzas and fish are also excellent, while the cheesecake with Amaretto is the star dessert. €€

Salvador

MAP PAGE 80, POCKET MAP G4
C/Barbieri 12 ⓦ casasalvadormadrid.com.
Ⓜ Chueca.
Chueca mainstay with bullfighting decor and simple, but well-cooked specials such as *rabo de toro* (bull's tail), *solomillo* (sirloin steak), stuffed peppers and *arroz con leche* (rice pudding). The set lunch offers.a good choice, and includes wine or beer. Closed August. €€

Zara

MAP PAGE 80, POCKET MAP F4
C/Barbieri 8 ⓦ restaurantezara.com.
Ⓜ Chueca or Gran Vía.
Excellent food for very good prices at this long-standing Cuban restaurant. *Ropa vieja* (strips of beef), fried yucca, minced beef with fried bananas and other specialities; the daiquiris are very good, too. €

Tapas bars

Baco y Beto

MAP PAGE 80, POCKET MAP F3
C/Pelayo 24 ⓦ baco-beto.com. Ⓜ Chueca.
Creative, delicious-tasting tapas in this small bar in the heart of Chueca. The constantly changing menu features a selection of wonderful flavours and fresh ingredients, and all at very reasonable prices. €

Bar Amor

MAP PAGE 80, POCKET MAP E1
C/Manuela Malasaña 22 ⓦ baramor.es.
Ⓜ San Bernardo or Bilbao.
This compact little corner restaurant has a carefully selected menu of appetising and appealingly presented *raciones* – think tuna

Museo Chicote on Gran Vía

in teriyaki sauce, or aubergine, courgette and goat's cheese salad. There is a good wine list too. €

Casa Julio

MAP PAGE 80, POCKET MAP E3
C/Madera 37 ☎ 915 227 273. Ⓜ Tribunal.
Famed for its *croquetas*, this old-style Madrid bar is nearly always full, and rightly so. The *croquetas* come in a range of flavours, from the traditional ham to spinach, leek and mushroom and blue cheese, the rest of the dishes are very good too. €

Celso y Manolo

MAP PAGE 80, POCKET MAP G10
C/Libertad 1 Ⓦ celsoymanolo.es. Ⓜ Chueca.
Named in honour of the original owners of an old *taberna* that used to occupy the site, entrepreneur Carlos Zamora has refurbished the bar while retaining the traditional fare, albeit with a contemporary twist. He has certainly succeeded, and the wide-ranging menu offers delicious *raciones* such as *croquetas de congrio* (conger eel croquettes), great rice dishes and a fantastic selection of Spanish tomato salads. €

Circo de las Tapas

MAP PAGE 80, POCKET MAP E4
C/Corredera Baja de San Pablo 21
Ⓦ circodelastapas.com. Ⓜ Callao or Tribunal.
This cosy bar-restaurant has a comprehensive offering of interesting tapas at competitive prices. Salads, garlic prawns, mussels and stuffed mushrooms are all popular, while the *tortilla* is outstanding. There is a good-value set lunch, paellas on Saturdays and brunch on Sunday. €

Gourmet Experience

MAP PAGE 80, POCKET MAP D10
El Corte Inglés, Plaza Callao 2 Ⓜ Callao.
Head for the ninth floor of this branch of the classic Spanish department store to enjoy some breathtaking views of Madrid. Gaze out over the Capitol building on the Gran Vía, the Palacio Real, and out towards the distant mountains as you sample a tapa, some oysters, a drink or an ice cream from one of the bars and food stalls set up on the top floor. €

Hermanos Vinagre

MAP PAGE 80, POCKET MAP G3
C/Gravina 17 Ⓦ hermanosvinagre.com.
Ⓜ Chueca.

Vibrant bar close to the plaza that's a favourite for an *aperitivo*. A range of *vermút*, including their own house variety and cold beers accompanied by *gildas* (marinated anchovies with a pickled pepper), tinned mussels or sardines. €

Mercado de San Antón

MAP PAGE 80, POCKET MAP G4
C/Augusto Figueroa 24
Ⓦ mercadosananton.com. Ⓜ Chueca.
Like the *Mercado San Miguel* near Plaza Mayor, this local market has become a trendy meeting place on the Chueca scene with gourmet foodstands, a wine bar, a café, a sushi stall and a stylish terrace bar on the top floor. €€

Pez Gordo

MAP PAGE 80, POCKET MAP E3
C/Pez 6 Ⓣ 915 223 208. Ⓜ Santo Domingo or Callao.
A fabulous array of tapas at this popular bar in this buzzing street north of Gran Vía. The grilled tuna, roast vegetables and tortilla are great options, but all the dishes are excellent. There is a good range of wines and beers on offer, the service is friendly and the prices are reasonable too. €

1862 Dry Bar

Pez Tortilla

MAP PAGE 80, POCKET MAP D3
C/Pez 36 Ⓦ peztortilla.com. Ⓜ Noviciado.
One of a small chain of bars specialising in *tortilla*, from the classic *tortilla de patatas* to varieties including goat's cheese, parmesan or *morcilla* (blood sausage), all of which are delicious. Also serves other snacks such as *croquetas*, *albondigas* (meatballs) and *patatas bravas*. €

Bars

1862 Dry Bar

MAP PAGE 80, POCKET MAP D3
C/Pez 27 Ⓦ facebook.com/1862DryBar.
Ⓜ Noviciado.
Expertly mixed and poured cocktails at this chic and compact two-floored watering hole in this bar-packed street north of Gran Vía. On the menu are the usual classics but also some signature cocktails developed by owner Alberto, all at very reasonable prices.

La Ardosa

MAP PAGE 80, POCKET MAP F3
C/Colón 13 Ⓦ bit.ly/LaArdosaMadrid.
Ⓜ Tribunal.
One of the city's classic *tabernas*, serving limited but delicious tapas including great *croquetas*, *salmorejo* and an excellent home-made *tortilla*. Also *vermút*, draught beer and Guinness.

Chicote

MAP PAGE 80, POCKET MAP F10
Gran Vía 12 Ⓦ museochicote.com.
Ⓜ Gran Vía.
Opened back in 1931 by Perico Chicote, ex-barman at the *Ritz*, Sophia Loren, Frank Sinatra, Ava Gardner, Luis Buñuel, Orson Welles and Hemingway have all passed through the doors of this cocktail bar. It's lost much of its old-style charm as it has tried to keep up to date, though it's still worth a visit for nostalgia's sake.

Del Diego

MAP PAGE 80, POCKET MAP F10
C/Reina 12 Ⓦ deldiego.com. Ⓜ Gran Vía.

New York-style cocktail bar set up by former *Chicote* waiter Fernando del Diego and now better than the original place. The expertly mixed cocktails are served up in a friendly, unhurried atmosphere. Margaritas, mojitos and Manhattans; the eponymously named vodka-based house special with advocaat and apricot brandy is a must. Closed August.

Fábrica Maravillas

MAP PAGE 80, POCKET MAP F3
C/Valverde 29 Ⓦ fmaravillas.com. Ⓜ Gran Vía or Tribunal.

Located in a fashionable, rejuvenated street running parallel to C/Fuencarral, Fábrica has helped promote the trend for craft beers in Madrid. An excellent collection of ales, including the fruity Malasaña, stout and a quality IPA.

Gin Club/Mercado de la Reina

MAP PAGE 80, POCKET MAP F10
Gran Vía 12 Ⓦ grupomercadodelareina.com. Ⓜ Gran Vía.

A tapas bar, restaurant and *bar de copas*. The bar serves a wide range of *pinchos* and *raciones* as well as a house special (upmarket) hamburger meal. The restaurant, serving up a wide range of traditional Spanish fare, is a little more pricey. At the back, with its mirrored ceilings and black leather chairs, the *Gin Club* cocktail bar offers over twenty different brands.

Gorila

MAP PAGE 80, POCKET MAP E3
Corredera Baja de San Pablo 47 Ⓦ facebook.com/Gorilamadrid. Ⓜ Chueca or Noviciado.

Eclectic design, mixing industrial-style furnishings with street art and neon lights, this bar has a chilled vibe, friendly staff and a great range of beers, spirits and cocktails. Happy hour is between 6 and 10pm from Sunday to Friday.

Propaganda 12

MAP PAGE 80, POCKET MAP G4
C/Libertad 12 Ⓦ propaganda12.com. Ⓜ Chueca.

The propaganda in question here is for Italian wines and food, and this sleek wine bar proselytizes to great effect. It is not cheap, but the wines are excellent, and the friendly staff are on hand to give advice. A small selection of Italian tapas and dishes are available, and they do a champagne breakfast on Sunday.

Taberna Ángel Sierra

MAP PAGE 80, POCKET MAP G3
C/Gravina 11 Ⓦ tabernadeangelsierra.es. Ⓜ chueca.

Perched on the edge of the plaza, this is one of the great bars in Madrid, where everyone drinks *vermút* accompanied by exquisite, free pickled anchovy tapas. *Raciones* are also available in the seated area, though they are a little pricey.

Clubs

BarCo

MAP PAGE 80, POCKET MAP E4
C/Barco 34 Ⓦ salabarco.com. Ⓜ Tribunal.

Popular venue in the midst of the increasingly fashionable Triball district, *BarCo* hosts regular concerts, flamenco and jam sessions, while the DJs take over late night with an eclectic selection of music – anything from the latest funk and hip hop to 80s classics (check website for schedules).

Tupperware

MAP PAGE 80, POCKET MAP F2
C/Corredera Alta de San Pablo 26 Ⓦ facebook.com/Tupperwarebar. Ⓜ Tribunal.

A Malasaña legend with retro decor and reasonably priced drinks, this is the place to go for indie tunes, with grunge and punk-era classics. Always packed downstairs, but a more relaxed atmosphere upstairs.

Salamanca and Paseo de la Castellana

Exclusive Barrio de Salamanca was developed in the second half of the nineteenth century as an upmarket residential zone under the patronage of the Marquis of Salamanca. Today, it's still home to Madrid's smartest apartments and designer emporiums, while the streets are populated by the chic clothes and sunglasses brigade, decked out in fur coats, Gucci and gold. Shopping aside, there's a scattering of sights here, including the pick of the city's smaller museums and Real Madrid's imposing Santiago Bernabéu stadium. Eateries are high-quality, but accordingly expensive. Bordering Salamanca to the west is the multi-lane Paseo de la Castellana, peppered with corporate office blocks, where, in summer, the section north of Plaza de Colón is littered with trendy terrazas.

Plaza de Colón

MAP PAGE 92, POCKET MAP H3
Ⓜ Colón.

Overlooking a busy crossroads and dominating the square in which they stand are a Neo-Gothic monument to Christopher Columbus (Cristóbal Colón), given as a wedding gift to Alfonso XII, and an enormous Spanish flag. Directly behind are the Jardines del Descubrimiento (Discovery Gardens), a small park containing three huge stone blocks representing Columbus's ships, the *Niña*, *Pinta* and *Santa María*. Below the plaza, underneath a cascading wall of water, is the **Teatro Fernán Gómez** (Ⓦ teatrofernangomez.es), a venue for theatre, film, dance, music and exhibitions.

Biblioteca Nacional and Museo del Libro

MAP PAGE 92, POCKET MAP J3
Paseo de Recoletos 20. Mon–Fri 9am–8pm. For exhibition opening hours check website. Free. Ⓦ bne.es. Ⓜ Colón.

The National Library contains several million volumes, including every work published in Spain since 1716. The museum within displays a selection of the library's treasures, including Arab, Hebrew and Greek manuscripts, and hosts regular temporary exhibitions related to the world of art and literature.

Museo Arqueológico Nacional

MAP PAGE 92, POCKET MAP J3
C/Serrano 13. Tues–Sat 9.30am–8pm, Sun 9.30am–3pm. Charge, free Sat after 2pm & Sun. Ⓦ man.es. Ⓜ Serrano or Colón.

A remarkable museum containing an outstanding collection of Iberian, Roman, Egyptian, Greek and Islamic finds, beautifully displayed around a naturally lit central atrium. Among the most impressive pieces, are the celebrated Celto-Iberian busts known as *La Dama de Elche* and *La Dama de Baza*, and a wonderfully rich hoard of Visigothic treasures found at Toledo.

Plaza de Toros de Las Ventas

Museo de Cera

MAP PAGE 92, POCKET MAP H3
Paseo de Recoletos 41. Daily:
April–Sept 11am–8pm, Oct–March
11am–7pm. Charge; discounts on website.
Ⓦ museoceramadrid.com. Ⓜ Colón.
Over 450 different personalities –
including a host of VIPs, heads of
state and, of course, Real Madrid
football stars – are displayed in
this expensive and kitsch museum,
which is nevertheless popular with
children. There's also a chamber
of horrors, a ghost train and a
history section.

Museo de Arte Público

MAP PAGE 92, POCKET MAP J1
Paseo de la Castellana 41 Ⓜ Rubén Darío.
An innovative use of the space
underneath the Juan Bravo flyover,
this open-air art museum is made
up of a haphazard collection
of sculptures, cubes, walls and
fountains, including work by
Eduardo Chillida, Joan Miró and
Julio González.

Museo Sorolla

MAP PAGE 92, POCKET MAP J1
Paseo del General Martínez Campos 37
Tues–Sat 9.30am–8pm, Sun 10am–3pm.
Charge, free Sat 2–8pm & Sun, and for
under-18s and over-65s. Ⓦ mecd.gob.
es/msorolla. Ⓜ Rubén Darío, Gregorio
Marañón or Iglesia.
Part museum and part art gallery,
this tribute to an artist's life and
work is one of Madrid's most
underrated treasures. Situated in
Joaquín Sorolla's former home,
it's a delightful oasis of peace and
tranquillity, its cool and shady
Andalucian-style courtyard and
gardens decked out with statues,
fountains, assorted plants and
fruit trees. The ground floor has
been kept largely intact, recreating
the authentic atmosphere of the
artist's living and working areas.
The upstairs rooms, originally the
sleeping quarters, have been turned
into a gallery, where sunlight, sea,
intense colours, women and children
dominate Sorolla's impressionistic
paintings. On your way out in the
Patio Andaluz, there's a collection of
his sketches and gouaches.

Museo Lázaro Galdiano

MAP PAGE 92, POCKET MAP J1
C/Serrano 122 Tues–Sun 9.30am–3pm.
Charge, free 2–3pm and for under-12s.
Ⓦ flg.es. Ⓜ Gregorio Marañón.

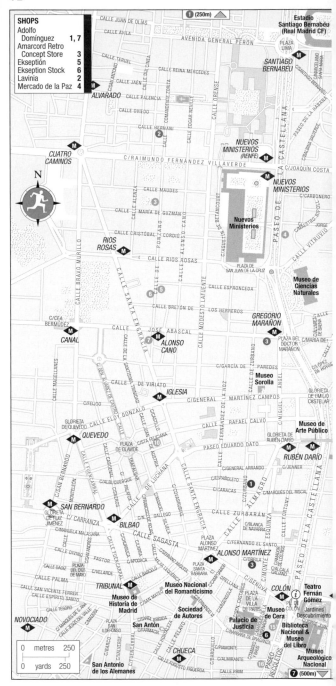

SHOPS
Adolfo Domínguez 1, 7
Amarcord Retro Concept Store 3
Ekseption 5
Ekseption Stock 6
Lavinia 2
Mercado de la Paz 4

93

Salamanca and Paseo de la Castellana

SALAMANCA AND PASEO DE LA CASTELLANA

ACCOMMODATION

ICON Embassy	5
Hotel Orfila	3
Hotel Santo Mauro	1
Hotel Único	2
Velázquez 45 By Pillow	4

CAFÉS

Café el Espejo	15
Café Gijón	16

RESTAURANTS

DiverXO	1
Gaudium	10
Hevia	8
El Invernadero	3
La Máquina	6
El Pescador	12
Le Qualité Tasca	5
Ramón Freixa Madrid	14
Sala de Despiece	7
La Tasquería	17
Ugo Chan	2

TAPAS BARS

Bar H Emblemático	11
Lateral	4, 9, 13

BAR

El Quinto Vino	2

CLUBS

Moby Dick	1
Opium	3

When businessman and publisher José Lázaro Galdiano died in 1947, he left his private collection – a vast treasure trove of paintings and objets d'art – to the state. Spread over the four floors of his former home, the collection contains jewellery, outstanding Spanish archeological pieces and some beautifully decorated thirteenth-century Limoges enamels. There's also an excellent selection of European paintings with works by Bosch, Rembrandt, Reynolds and Constable, plus Spanish artists including Zurbarán, Velázquez, El Greco and Goya. Other exhibits include several clocks and watches, many of them once owned by Emperor Charles V.

Museo de Ciencias Naturales

MAP PAGE 92, POCKET MAP J1
C/José Gutiérrez Abascal 2. Tues–Fri 10am–5pm, Sat & Sun 10am–8pm (July & Aug 10am–3pm). Charge, free Sun 5–8pm. Ⓦ mncn.csic.es. Ⓜ Gregorio Marañón.
The Natural History Museum's displays are split between two buildings. One contains a fairly predictable collection of stuffed animals, skeletons and audio-visual displays on the evolution of life on earth and biodiversity, the other is home to some rather dull fossil and geological exhibits.

Estadio Santiago Bernabéu

MAP PAGE 92, POCKET MAP J1
C/Concha Espina 1. Tour and trophy exhibition: Mon–Sat 9.30am–6.30pm, Sun 10.30am–6.30pm; check website for changes on match days. Charge. Ⓦ realmadrid.com. Ⓜ Santiago Bernabéu.
The magnificent, recently modernised, 80,000-seater Bernabéu stadium provides a suitably imposing home for one of the most glamorous teams in football, Real Madrid. Venue of the 1982 World Cup final, the stadium has witnessed countless triumphs of "Los blancos", who have notched up 35 Spanish league titles and 14 European Cup triumphs in their 117-year history. Real have had some of the biggest names in football on their books including Alfredo Di Stefano, Luis Figo, Zinedine Zidane, Ronaldo, David Beckham, Cristiano Ronaldo, Luka Modric and Gareth Bale. Tickets for big games can be tricky to get hold of, but the website has all the details.

You can catch a glimpse of the hallowed turf on the exorbitantly-priced stadium tour during which you visit the changing rooms, walk around the edge of the pitch and sit in the VIP box before heading to the trophy room with its endless cabinets of gleaming silverware. The tour ends with the obligatory visit to the club shop – where you soon come to realize why Real is one of the richest football clubs in the world.

Plaza Castilla

MAP PAGE 92, POCKET MAP J1
Ⓜ Plaza de la Castilla.
The Paseo de la Castellana ends with a flourish at Plaza Castilla with the dramatic leaning towers of the Puerta de Europa and four giant

Plaza Castilla

skyscrapers constructed on Real Madrid's former training ground, the result of a controversial deal that allowed the club to solve many of its financial problems. The two tallest towers – one by Norman Foster – soar some 250 metres skywards.

Plaza de Toros de Las Ventas

MAP PAGE 92, POCKET MAP K3
C/Alcalá 237 Tours: daily April–Oct 10am–6pm, Nov–March 10am–5pm. Charge; tickets at Ⓦ lasventastour.com; tickets for bullfights available through the website. Ⓦ las-ventas.info. Ⓜ Ventas.

On the easternmost tip of the Barrio de Salamanca, Madrid's 23,000-capacity, Neo-Mudéjar bullring, Las Ventas, is the most illustrious in the world. The season lasts from March to October and *corridas* (bullfights) are held every Sunday at 7pm and every day during the three main *ferias* (fairs): La Comunidad (early May), San Isidro (mid-May to June) and Otoño (late Sept to Oct). Tickets go on sale at the ring a couple of days in advance, though many are already allocated to season-ticket holders. The cheapest seats are *andanadas* and *gradas*, the highest rows at the back; the front rows are known as the *tendidos bajos* or *barreras*. Seats are also divided into *sol* (sun), *sombra* (shade) and *sol y*

Museo Arqueológico Nacional

sombra (shaded after a while), with *sombra* the most expensive.

There's a refurbished taurine **museum** attached to the bullring (daily 10am–3pm; free) with an intriguing collection of memorabilia including stunning *trajes de luces*, the beautifully decorated suits worn by the *toreros*. As well as stepping out onto the sand yourself you can visit the medical room where injured *toreros* are treated and the chapel where they pray beforehand.

Bullfighting

The bullfight is a classic image of Spain, but the ethical arguments against it are well-known – the governments of Catalunya and the Canary Islands have gone so far as to ban it. Spain's main opposition to bullfighting is organised by ADDA (Ⓦ addaong.org), whose website has information about international campaigns and current actions. To aficionados, the bulls are a ritual part of Spanish culture, with the emphasis on the way man and bull "perform" together. Fighting bulls are, they will tell you, bred for the industry; they live a reasonable life before they are killed, and if the bullfight went, so, too, would the bulls. If you decide to attend a *corrida*, try to see a big, prestigious event, where star performers are likely to despatch the bulls with "art" and a "clean" kill; there are few sights worse than a matador making a prolonged, messy kill.

Shops

Adolfo Domínguez

MAP PAGE 92, POCKET MAP J4
C/Serrano 5 ⓦ adolfodominguez.com.
Ⓜ Retiro.

Domínguez has a massive five-storey flagship store for his slightly sober but elegant modern Spanish designs – a wide range of natural colours and free lines for both men and women. There is another branch at C/Serrano 40.

Amarcord Retro Concept Store

MAP PAGE 92, POCKET MAP K1
C/Don Ramón de la Cruz 47 ⓦ amarcord-store.com. Ⓜ Lista or Nuñez de Balboa.

Named after the nostalgic Fellini film, this lovely shop is a homage to the past with a selection of antiques and curios as well as new goods such as stationery, fashion accessories and cosmetics. Good for original gifts.

Ekseptión

MAP PAGE 92, POCKET MAP K3 & H3
C/Velázquez 28 ⓦ ekseption.com.
Ⓜ Velázquez.

Café el Espejo

A dramatic catwalk bathed in spotlights leads into this shop selling some of the most expensive women's clothes in Madrid. For slightly cheaper options try Ekseption Stock at C/Marqués de la Ensenada 2, which sells discounted lines.

Lavinia

MAP PAGE 92, POCKET MAP K1
C/José Ortega y Gasset 16 ⓦ lavinia.com.
Ⓜ Nuñez de Balboa.

A massive wine shop with a great selection from Spain and the rest of the world. The perfect place to get that Ribera del Duero, Albariño or Rueda that you wanted to take home.

Mercado de la Paz

MAP PAGE 92, POCKET MAP K2
C/Ayala 28 ⓦ mercadodelapaz.com.
Ⓜ Serrano.

High-end food market with some great stalls, bars, restaurants and the delicatessen *La Boulette* which, amongst other delights, offers a fantastic selection of cheeses.

Cafés

Café el Espejo

MAP PAGE 92, POCKET MAP H3
Paseo de Recoletos 31
ⓦ grancafeelespejo.com. Ⓜ Colón.

Opened in 1990, but you wouldn't guess it from the antiquated decor – think mirrors, gilt and a wonderful, extravagant glass pavilion. The leafy terraza is an ideal spot to enjoy a coffee and watch the world go by. €€

Café Gijón

MAP PAGE 92, POCKET MAP H4
Paseo de Recoletos 21 ⓦ cafegijon.com.
Ⓜ Colón.

A famous literary café dating from 1888, decked out in Cuban mahogany and mirrors. A centre of the *Movida* in the 1980s, it still hosts regular artistic *tertulias* (discussion groups). There is a restaurant, but you're better off

Lavinia wine shop

sticking to drinks in the bar or on the pleasant summer terraza. €€

Restaurants

DiverXO

MAP PAGE 92, POCKET MAP J1
C/Padre Damián 23 Ⓦ diverxo.com.
Ⓜ Cuzco.

Madrid's only three-Michelin-star restaurant, located in the *NH Eurobuilding* hotel, is run by chef Dabid Muñoz and has a reputation for avant-garde cuisine, stunning presentation and mouth-watering food. Prices are astronomical – taster menus cost a minimum of €365 and that is without drinks! The waiting list is long, so there are clearly some who can afford the experience. You have to book 90 days in advance, paying a per head charge which is discounted from the final bill. €€€€

Gaudium

MAP PAGE 92, POCKET MAP G1
C/Santa Feliciana 14 Ⓦ gaudiumchamberi.com.
Ⓜ Iglesia.

Quality ingredients, good service and a selection of simple dishes with a creative twist served up in this intimate restaurant close to the popular Plaza de Olavide. Offerings include grilled vegetables, oxtail with grapes and cod with garlic, basil and dried tomato. €€€

Hevia

MAP PAGE 92, POCKET MAP J1
C/Serrano 118 Ⓦ heviamadrid.com.
Ⓜ Rubén Darío or Gregorio Marañón.

Plush venue for plush clientele feasting on pricey but excellent tapas and canapés – the guacamole with anchovies is delicious, as is the selection of smoked fish – as well as full meals in the restaurant. €€€

El Invernadero

MAP PAGE 92, POCKET MAP G1
C/Ponzano 85 Ⓦ elinvernaderorestaurante.com. Ⓜ Nuevos Ministerios.

Superb quality vegetarian, fish, meat and non-gluten options are available in this small, Michelin-starred restaurant where you get a chance to see the chefs at work and then to hear them explain their creations. The *menú verde* is vegetarian, *rojo* contains meat and *azul* includes fish; dishes are beautifully presented and taste exquisite. €€€€

La Máquina

MAP PAGE 92, POCKET MAP G1

C/Ponzano 39–41 ⓦ lamaquinachamberi.es.
ⓂRíos Rosas.

Three different spaces in this sleek
eatery: the bar and terrace areas
serve up a great range of *pinchos*,
tapas and *raciones* including
excellent fried fish, while the
restaurant at the back is for more
formal meals with rice dishes, stews
and quality meat and fish. €€€

El Pescador

MAP PAGE 92, POCKET MAP K1

C/José Ortega y Gasset 75
ⓦ marisqueriaelpescador.net. Ⓜ Lista.

One of the city's top seafood
restaurants, with specials flown in
daily from the Atlantic. Prices are
high, but you'll rarely experience
better-quality seafood than this. If
funds don't stretch to a full meal,
you can try a *ración* in the bar
instead. Closed August. €€€€

Le Qualité Tasca

MAP PAGE 92, POCKET MAP G1

C/Ponzano 48 ⓦ lequalitetasca.com.
ⓂRíos Rosas.

Small restaurant in this popular
bar-heavy street, which has won

Mercado de la Paz

plaudits for its *patatas bravas* and
cheesecake. The crunchy slices
of *morcilla* with apple, brie and
mango are delicious and the lamb
meatballs and wild cod are also very
good. €€€

Ramón Freixa Madrid

MAP PAGE 92, POCKET MAP J2

C/Claudio Coello 67 ⓦ ramonfreixamadrid.com.
ⓂSerrano.

Catalan chef Ramón Freixa's
flagship Michelin-star restaurant
in Madrid is situated in the
luxury surroundings of the *Hotel
Único* (see page 133) in the
heart of Salamanca. Creative and
impeccably presented dishes from
an ever-changing menu featuring
superb game, fish and new twists
on Spanish classics. There are
several taster menus, ranging
in prices (wine extra). Only has
space for 35 diners, so book well
in advance, especially if you want
a table on the summer terrace.
Closed Easter and August. €€€€

Sala de Despiece

MAP PAGE 92, POCKET MAP G1

C/Ponzano 11 ⓦ saladedespiece.com.
ⓂAlonso Cano.

Despiece means cutting up into pieces
and the concept behind this bar is
that high quality raw material is
king. Inside, there is just one long,
white bar lined with stools and
eating feels more like a tasting session
rather than a meal. On offer is a
selection of supremely tasty hand-
picked ingredients pared down to
the essentials and delivered on plastic
or metal trays. Arrive unfashionably
early or be prepared for a long wait
for a slot at the bar. €€

La Tasquería

MAP PAGE 92, POCKET MAP K1

C/Duque de Sesto 48 ⓦ latasqueria.com.
ⓂGoya.

Offal is the central ingredient of
most of the dishes at *La Tasquería*,
whether it comes from pigs, cows,
lamb, duck or rabbit. Sweetbread
ravioli, duck heart with raspberry

and pork cheek with red prawns give an idea of what is on offer. There is a selection of taster menus available too. €€€

Ugo Chan

MAP PAGE 92, POCKET MAP G1
C/Félix Bois 6 Ⓦ ugochan.com.
Ⓜ Plaza Castilla.

Japanese fusion-style food at this top-quality restaurant in the north of Madrid. A seasonal menu featuring sashimi, red tuna tartare, *nigiri* sushi and *gyoza*. Excellent quality ingredients and attentive service. €€€€

Tapas bars

Bar H Emblemático

MAP PAGE 92, POCKET MAP J1
C/Castelló 83 Ⓦ barhemblematico.es.
Ⓜ Nuñez de Balboa.

Cozy, reasonably priced bar with some simple, but excellent quality tapas on offer, the *molletes* (a sort of open sandwich) – *calamares*, *jamón* and *tortilla* – are a house speciality, but the *patatas brava* and *chistorra* (spicy sausage from Navarra) are also very good. €

Lateral

MAP PAGE 92, POCKET MAP J1 AND K1
Paseo de la Castellana 42 Ⓦ lateral.com.
Ⓜ Rubén Darío.

A swish easy-going tapas bar chain serving classic dishes such as *croquetas* and *pimientos rellenos* (stuffed peppers) with a modern twist. There are other branches at C/Velázquez 57, C/Fuencarral 43, Paseo de la Castellana 89 and Plaza Santa Ana 12.

Bar

El Quinto Vino

MAP PAGE 92, POCKET MAP G1
C/Hernani 48 Ⓦ elquintovino.com.
Ⓜ Nuevos Ministerios or Cuatro Caminos.

Superb home-made *croquetas*, *huevos estrellados* and *rabo de toro*

Café Gijón

with a great selection of wines in this very popular bar just behind Nuevos Ministerios. They also do a decent traditional set lunch. €€

Clubs

Moby Dick

MAP PAGE 92, POCKET MAP J1
Avda Brasil 5 Ⓦ mobydickclub.com.
Ⓜ Cuzco or Santiago Bernabéu.

Intimate club/music venue with a friendly atmosphere. Plays host to a variety of Spanish groups and the odd international star, and the music ranges from indie to pop-rock and jazz.

Opium

MAP PAGE 92, POCKET MAP J1
C/José Abascal 56 Ⓦ opiummadrid.com.
Ⓜ Gregorio Marañón.

Electronic/house music from resident DJs in this reopened club (its predecessor was closed for exceeding maximum capacity). Popular with *pijos* – fashion-conscious rich kids – and the upmarket glamour crowd. Cover charge includes the first drink; often free entry before 1.30am.

Plaza de España and beyond

Largely constructed in the Franco era and dominated by two early Spanish skyscrapers, the Plaza de España provides an imposing full stop to Gran Vía and a breathing space from the densely packed streets to the east. Beyond the square lies a mixture of aristocratic suburbia, university campus and parkland, distinguished by the green swathes of Parque del Oeste and Casa de Campo. Sights include the eclectic collections of the Museo Cerralbo, the fascinating Museo de América, the Ermita de San Antonio de la Florida, with its stunning Goya frescoes and, further out, the pleasant royal residence of El Pardo. Meanwhile, the spacious terrazas along Paseo del Pintor Rosales and the bars and restaurants scattered throughout the area provide ample opportunity for refreshment.

Plaza de España

MAP PAGE 102, POCKET MAP C3
Ⓜ Plaza de España.

The Plaza de España was the Spanish dictator Franco's attempt to portray Spain as a dynamic, modern country. The gargantuan, iconic **Edificio de España**, which heads the square, looks like it was transplanted from 1920s New York, but was in fact completed in 1953. Four years later, the 32-storey **Torre de Madrid** took over for some time as the tallest building in Spain. Both buildings have been converted into luxury hotels, and

Plaza de España

together they tower over the newly
spruced-up plaza, which is centred
around the emblematic monument
to Cervantes.

Museo de Cerralbo

MAP PAGE 102, POCKET MAP B3
C/Ventura Rodríguez 17. Tues, Wed, Fri &
Sat 9.30am–3pm, Thurs 9.30am–3pm &
5–8pm, Sun & hols 10am–3pm. Charge,
free Thurs 5–8pm, Sat after 2pm, Sun, for
under-18s and over-65s. ⓦ bit.ly/Cerralbo.
Ⓜ Plaza de España.

Reactionary politician, poet,
traveller and archeologist, the
seventeenth Marqués de Cerralbo
endowed his elegant nineteenth-
century mansion with a substantial
collection of paintings, furniture
and armour. Bequeathed to
the state on his death, the
house opened as a museum in
1962 and the cluttered nature of
the exhibits is partly explained
by the fact that the marqués' will
stipulated that objects should
be displayed exactly as he had
arranged them. Among the art on
show are works by Tintoretto, El
Greco and Goya, but the highlight
is a fabulous over-the-top mirrored
ballroom with a Tiepolo-inspired
fresco, golden stuccowork and
marbled decoration.

Nomad Museo

MAP PAGE 102, POCKET MAP C3
Gran Vía 78. Mon–Thurs & Sun 10am–10pm,
Fri & Sat 10am–midnight. Charge.
ⓦ nomadmuseo.es. Ⓜ Plaza España
Digital technology to the fore
in this experiential museum
with visually impressive 360°
projections and virtual reality
activities. Popular with children,
but relatively small and rather
over-priced, the inaugural Utopia
exhibition imagines a universe
directed by artificial intelligence.

Centro Cultural
Conde Duque

MAP PAGE 102, POCKET MAP C2
C/Conde Duque 9–11 ⓦ condedquemadrid.es.
Ⓜ Ventura Rodríguez.

Centro Cultural Conde Duque

Constructed in the early eighteenth
century, this former royal guard
barracks has been converted into a
dynamic cultural centre, housing the
city's **contemporary art** collection
(Tues–Fri 10am–2pm & 3–9pm,
Sat 10am–2pm & 5.30–9pm, Sun
10.30am–2.30pm; free), a recreation
of the study of early twentieth-
century writer Ramón Gómez de
la Serna and hosting a variety of
exhibitions and concerts.

Plaza de las
Comendadoras

MAP PAGE 102, POCKET MAP D2
Ⓜ Noviciado.
Bordered by a variety of interesting
craft shops, bars and cafés, this
tranquil square is named after the
convent that occupies one side
of it. The convent is run by nuns
from the military order of Santiago
and the attached church is decked
out with banners celebrating the
victories of the Order's knights.
A large painting of their patron,
St James the Moor-slayer, hangs
over the high altar. The plaza itself
comes alive in the summer months
when the terrazas open and locals
gather for a chat and a drink.

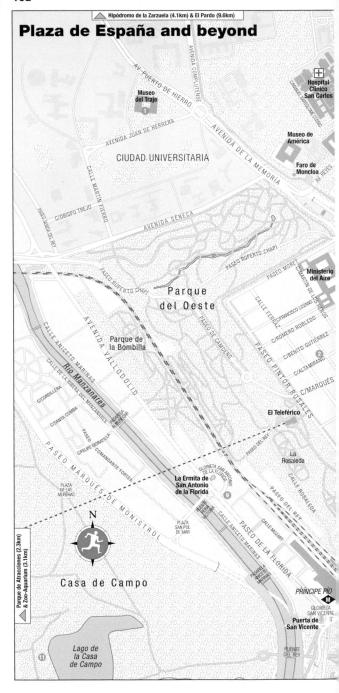

Plaza de España and beyond

Hipódromo de la Zarzuela (4.1km) & El Pardo (9.6km)

AVENIDA COMPLUTENSE

AV. PUERTO DE HIERRO

AVENIDA JUAN DE HERRERA

Museo del Traje ❶

CALLE MARTÍN FIERRO

PASEO SENDA DEL REY

C/OBISPO TREJO

CIUDAD UNIVERSITARIA

AVENIDA DE LA MEMORIA

Hospital Clínico San Carlos

CARMEN RODRÍGUEZ LOSADA

Museo de América

Faro de Moncloa

AV. REYES

AVENIDA SÉNECA

PASEO RUPERTO CHAPÍ

Parque del Oeste

PASEO RUPERTO CHAPÍ

PASEO MORET

Ministerio del Aire

C/MARTÍN DE LOS HEROS

CALLE FERRAZ

C/FRANCISCO LOZANO

C/ROMERO ROBLEDO

C/BENITO GUTIÉRREZ

C/ALTAMIRANO ❷

C/MARQUÉS

PASEO DE CAMOENS

PASEO PINTOR ROSALES

CALLE ANICETO MARINAS

AVENIDA VALLADOLID

Parque de la Bombilla

Río Manzanares

C/CORDILLERA

CALLE DE LA RIBERA DEL MANZANARES

C/SANTA COMBA

PASEO DE LA RIBERA DEL MANZANARES

El Teleférico

C/FELIPE MORATILLA

La Rosaleda

PASEO DEL REY

PLAZA DE LAS MORERAS

PASEO MARQUÉS DE MONISTROL

PASEO COMANDANTE FORTEA

Glorieta San Antonio de la Florida

La Ermita de San Antonio de la Florida ❾

CALLE ROSALEDA

PASEO DE LA FLORIDA

PLAZA SAN POL DE MAR

PUENTE DE LA REINA VICTORIA

CALLE ANICETO MARINAS

CALLE MOZART

PASEO DEL REY

N

Parque de Atracciones (2.3km) & Zoo-Aquarium (3.1km)

Casa de Campo

PASARELA ARCO RETIRO

PRÍNCIPE PÍO Ⓜ

GLORIETA SAN VICENTE

Puerta de San Vicente

PUENTE DEL REY

Lago de la Casa de Campo ⓫

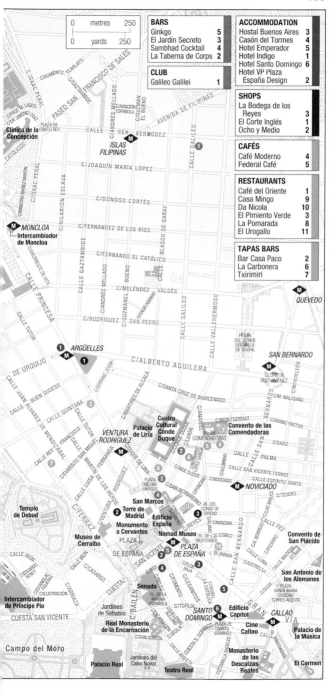

BARS	
Ginkgo	5
El Jardín Secreto	3
Sambhad Cocktail	4
La Taberna de Corps	2

CLUB	
Galileo Galilei	1

ACCOMMODATION	
Hostal Buenos Aires	3
Casón del Tormes	4
Hotel Emperador	5
Hotel Indigo	1
Hotel Santo Domingo	6
Hotel VP Plaza	
España Design	2

SHOPS	
La Bodega de los Reyes	3
El Corte Inglés	1
Ocho y Medio	2

CAFÉS	
Café Moderno	4
Federal Café	5

RESTAURANTS	
Café del Oriente	1
Casa Mingo	9
Da Nicola	10
El Pimiento Verde	3
La Pomarada	8
El Urogallo	11

TAPAS BARS	
Bar Casa Paco	2
La Carbonera	6
Txirimiri	7

Faro de Moncloa

Spanish Conquest, as well as more recent acquisitions and donations. The layout is thematic, with sections on geography, history, social organization, religion and communication. The Aztec, Maya and Inca civilizations are well represented, and exhibits include the Madrid Codex, one of only three surviving hieroglyphic manuscripts depicting everyday Maya life; the Tudela Codex, with indigenous paintings describing the events of the Spanish Conquest; and the Quimbayas Treasure, a breathtaking collection of gold objects from a funeral treasure of the Colombian Quimbaya culture, dated 900–600 BC.

Faro de Moncloa

MAP PAGE 102, POCKET MAP B1
Avenida de los Reyes Católicos 6. Tues–Sun 9.30am–8pm. Charge, free for under-7se. Ⓜ Moncloa, take the Plaza de Moncloa exit.
Next to the Museo de América is Faro de Moncloa, a futuristic 110-metre-high viewing tower which has reopened after an eleven-year closure. Originally built in 1992 by architect Salvador Pérez Arroyo, when Madrid was named European City of Culture, the tower offers fantastic views over the city, Casa de Campo and out towards the mountains.

Ministerio del Aire

MAP PAGE 102, POCKET MAP B1
Ⓜ Moncloa.
The Air Ministry is a product of the post-Civil War Francoist building boom. Work on the mammoth edifice began in 1942, and even the Third Reich's architect, Albert Speer, was consulted. However, with the defeat of the Nazis, plans were soon changed, and a Habsburg-style structure was built instead – nicknamed the "Monasterio" del Aire because of its similarity to El Escorial (see page 119). The neighbouring Arco de la Victoria was constructed in 1956 to commemorate the Nationalist military triumph in the Civil War.

Museo del Traje

MAP PAGE 102, POCKET MAP B1
Avda de Juan de Herrera 2. Tues–Sat 9.30am–7pm, Sun & hols 10am–3pm (July & Aug open until 10.30pm Thurs). Charge, free, Sat after 2.30pm, all day Sun, for under-18s and over-65s. Ⓦ bit.ly/Traje. Ⓜ Moncloa.
A fascinating excursion through the history of clothes and costume. Exhibits include garments from a royal tomb dating back to the thirteenth century, some stunning eighteenth-century ballgowns and a selection of Spanish regional costumes as well as shoes, jewellery and underwear. Modern Spanish and international designers are

Museo de América

MAP PAGE 102, POCKET MAP B1
Avda de los Reyes Católicos. Tues, Wed, Fri & Sat 9.30am–3pm, Thurs 9.30am–7pm, Sun 10am–3pm. Charge, free Thurs after 2pm, Sun, and for under-18s, students and over-65s. Ⓦ bit.ly/MuseoAmerica. Ⓜ Moncloa.
This fabulous collection of pre-Columbian American art and artefacts includes objects brought back at the time of the

also featured, with a Paco Rabane mini-skirt and elegant shoes from Pedro del Hierro. There is an upmarket restaurant in the grounds, *Café del Oriente*, which has a cool garden terrace in the summer (see page 109).

Parque del Oeste

MAP PAGE 102, POCKET MAP A2–B3
Ⓜ Moncloa.

Featuring a pleasant stream, assorted statues and shady walks, this delightful park offers a welcome respite from the busy streets of the capital. There are also remains of some of the bunkers used to defend the city when Franco's rebel nationalist forces laid siege to the city in the Civil War. In summer, there are numerous terrazas overlooking it on Paseo del Pintor Rosales. The beautiful rose garden (daily 10am–dusk) – in Calle de la Rosaleda – is at its most fragrant in May and June, while further down the hill is a small cemetery where the 43 Spaniards – executed by occupying French troops on May 3, 1808, and immortalized by Goya in his famous painting in the Prado (see page 64) – lie buried.

Templo de Debod

MAP PAGE 102, POCKET MAP B3
C/Ferraz 1. Tues–Sun 10am–7pm. Free.
Ⓦ madrid.es/templodebod. Ⓜ Plaza de España.

A fourth-century BC Egyptian temple in the middle of Madrid may seem an incongruous sight. It's here, however, as a thank-you from the Egyptian government for Spanish help in salvaging archeological sites threatened by the construction of the Aswan High Dam. Reconstructed here stone by stone in 1968, it has a multi-media exhibition on the culture of Ancient Egypt inside. Archeologists have called for it to be enclosed and insulated from the open air as pollution is taking a heavy toll on the stone.

El Teleférico

MAP PAGE 102, POCKET MAP A2
Paseo del Pintor Rosales. April–Sept Mon–Fri noon–dusk (exact times vary), Sat & Sun noon–around 8pm; Oct–March Sat, Sun & hols noon–dusk. Charge, under-4s free.
Ⓦ teleferico.emtmadrid.es. Ⓜ Argüelles.

The Teleférico **cable car** shuttles passengers from the edge of the Parque del Oeste high over the

PLAZA DE ESPAÑA AND BEYOND

El Teleférico over the Parque del Oeste

Manzanares river to a restaurant/bar in the middle of Casa de Campo (see page 106). The round trip offers some fine views of the park, the Palacio Real, the Almudena cathedral and the city skyline.

La Ermita de San Antonio de la Florida

MAP PAGE 102, POCKET MAP A4
Paseo de la Florida 5. Mid-Sept to mid-June Tues–Sun 9.30am–8pm; mid-June to mid-Sept Tues–Fri 9.30am–2pm & 3–7pm, Sat & Sun 9.30am–7pm; guided tours on Sat 1pm. Free. ⓦ madrid.es/ermita. Ⓜ Príncipe Pío.

Built on a Greek-cross plan between 1792 and 1798, this little church is the burial site of Goya and also features some outstanding frescoes by the artist. Those in the dome depict St Anthony of Padua resurrecting a dead man to give evidence in favour of a prisoner (the saint's father) unjustly accused of murder. The *ermita* also houses Goya's mausoleum, although his head was stolen by phrenologists for examination in the nineteenth century. The mirror-image chapel on the other side of the road was built in 1925 for parish services so that the original could become a museum. On St Anthony's Day (June 13), girls queue at the church to ask the saint for a boyfriend; if pins dropped into the holy water then stick to their hands, their wish will be granted.

Casa de Campo

MAP PAGE 102, POCKET MAP A4
Ⓜ Lago.

The Casa de Campo, an enormous expanse of heath and scrub, is in parts surprisingly wild for a place so easily accessible from the city. Founded by Felipe II in the mid-sixteenth century as a royal hunting estate, it was only opened to the public in 1931 and soon after acted as a base for Franco's forces to shell the city. Large sections have been tamed for conventional pastimes and there are picnic tables and café/bars throughout the park, the ones by the lake providing fine views of the city. There are also mountain bike trails, a jogging track, an open-air swimming pool (June–Sept daily 11am–9pm; charge), tennis courts and rowing boats for rent on the lake, all near Metro Lago. The park is best avoided after dark as many of its roads are frequented by prostitutes.

Zoo-Aquarium

MAP PAGE 102, POCKET MAP A4
Casa de Campo. Daily 10.30/11am–dusk. Charge, under-3s free; discounts via website. ⓦ zoomadrid.com. Ⓜ Batán.

Laid out in sections corresponding to the five continents, Madrid's zoo, on the southwestern edge of Casa de Campo, provides decent enclosures and plenty of space for over two thousand different species – though of course all of the usual animal welfare concerns about zoos apply here too. When you've had your fill of big cats, pandas, koalas and venomous snakes, you can check out the aquarium, dolphinarium, children's zoo or bird show. Boats

Parque de Atracciones

can be rented and there are mini-train tours.

Parque de Atracciones

MAP PAGE 102, POCKET MAP A4
Casa de Campo. April–Sept most days noon–8/9pm (midnight on Sat & in July & Aug); Oct–March weekends and hols noon–7pm. Charge, children under 1m tall free; significant discounts via website. ⓦ parquedeatracciones.es. ⓜ Batán.

This is Madrid's most popular **theme park**, where highlights for adults and teenagers include the 100km/h Abismo rollercoaster, the swirling Tarantula ride, the 63-metre vertical drop La Lanzadera, the stomach-churning La Máquina and the whitewater raft ride Los Rápidos. There are some more sedate attractions too, as well as an area for younger children. Spanish acts perform in the open-air auditorium in the summer and there are frequent parades too, plus plenty of burger/pizza places to replace lost stomach contents.

Hipódromo de la Zarzuela

MAP PAGE 102, POCKET MAP A4
Carretera La Coruña km 8. Charge, under-14s free. There is a free bus that leaves Paseo de Moret next to the Intercambiador in Moncloa in the two hours before the races, returning up to an hour after they finish. ⓦ hipodromodelazarzuela.es.

The **horseracing** track just out of the city on the A Coruña road holds races every Sunday in the spring and autumn, and on Thursday and Saturday evenings in July. If you enjoy horseracing (bearing in mind the usual ethical issues involved), you'll find that the unstuffy atmosphere and beautiful setting can make this a fun day out for all the family.

El Pardo

MAP PAGE 102, POCKET MAP A4
C/Manuel Alonso. Tues–Sun 10am–7pm. Charge, free Wed & Sun 3–7pm. Buses (#601) from Moncloa (daily 6.30am–midnight; every 10–15min; 25min). ⓦ patrimonionacional.es.

Hipódromo de la Zarzuela

Nine kilometres northwest of central Madrid lies Franco's former principal residence at El Pardo. A garrison still remains at the town, where most of the Generalíssimo's staff were based, but the place is now a popular excursion for *madrileños*, who come here for long lunches at the excellent terraza restaurants. The tourist focus is the **Palacio del Pardo**, rebuilt by the Bourbons on the site of the hunting lodge of Carlos I and still used by visiting heads of state. Behind the imposing but blandly symmetrical facade, the interior houses the chapel where Franco prayed, and the theatre where he used to censor films. On display are a number of mementos of the dictator, including his desk, a portrait of Isabel la Católica and an excellent collection of tapestries. With its highly ornate interior, the country house retreat known as the Casita del Príncipe, designed by Prado architect Juan de Villanueva for Carlos IV and his wife María Luisa de Parma, is also open for visits by appointment only (☎ 913 761 500; charge).

Casa Mingo

Shops

La Bodega de los Reyes

MAP PAGE 102, POCKET MAP D3
C/Reyes 6 Ⓦ labodegadelosreyes.com.
Ⓜ Plaza de España.
Established wine shop with an
excellent selection of Spanish
produce. They also offer
competitively priced tasting
sessions in the cellar room with
accompanying tapas.

El Corte Inglés

MAP PAGE 102, POCKET MAP B1
C/Princesa 41, 47 & 56 Ⓦ elcorteingles.es.
Ⓜ Argüelles.
One of many branches of
Spain's biggest and most
popular department store. It
stocks everything from souvenirs
and gift items to clothes and
electrical goods. Prices are on the
high side, but quality is usually
very good.

Ocho y Medio

MAP PAGE 102, POCKET MAP C3
C/Martín de los Heros 11
Ⓦ ochoymediolibrosdecine.es. Ⓜ Plaza
de España.

Fascinating cinema bookshop with
a pleasantly anarchic collection
of books and film-star-backed
products, as well as a great terrace
and small café. Perfect for a stop
before watching one of the original-
version films in the nearby cinemas.

Cafés

Café Moderno

MAP PAGE 102, POCKET MAP D2
Plaza de las Comendadoras 1 Ⓜ Noviciado.
Relaxing café-bar serving good-
value drinks, snacks and evening
cocktails with a busy summer
terraza, situated on one of the city's
nicest squares. There are two other
decent café-bars alongside if this
one is too crowded. €

Federal Café

MAP PAGE 102, POCKET MAP D2
Plaza de las Comendadoras 9
Ⓦ federalcafe.es. Ⓜ Plaza España.
Laid-back, spacious café with large
windows looking out onto a
pleasant plaza. *Federal* serves up
good coffee, breakfasts and snacks,
although service can be a bit hit
and miss. With its free wi-fi and

large tables, it's just the place to catch up on your emails, do some work or read the paper. €

Restaurants

Café del Oriente

MAP PAGE 102, POCKET MAP B1
Avda. Juan de Herrera 2
Ⓦ cafedeorientemuseodeltraje.com.
Ⓜ Ciudad Universitaria.

Situated in the delightful pine-fringed grounds of the Museo del Traje, the setting is the big draw of this restaurant. The set lunch is quite good value, but an evening meal featuring dishes such as hake with artichoke and *alioli*, or steak with plum sauce will set you back a good deal more. €€€

Casa Mingo

MAP PAGE 102, POCKET MAP A4
Paseo de la Florida 34 Ⓦ casamingo.es.
Ⓜ Príncipe Pío.

Crowded and reasonably priced Asturian chicken-and-cider house – you'll need to arrive early or hang around for a table on the terrace in good weather. The spit-roast chicken is practically compulsory,

though the chorizo cooked in cider and *cabrales* (blue cheese) is also very good. Closed August. €

Da Nicola

MAP PAGE 102, POCKET MAP D3
Plaza Mostenses 11 Ⓦ danicola.es. Ⓜ Plaza de España.

Popular Italian restaurant with an extensive range of pizzas, pastas and meat dishes all at reasonable prices; the gnocchi filled with cheese and pesto is particularly good. A good option for families. Gluten-free dishes available. €

El Pimiento Verde

MAP PAGE 102, POCKET MAP B2
C/Quintana 1 Ⓦ elpimientoverde.com.
Ⓜ Argüelles or Ventura Rodríguez.

Friendly Basque restaurant renowned for its artichoke flowers, stuffed peppers, rice with lobster and flame-grilled steak. Mains are quite expensive, but many of the dishes can be shared as the portions are generous. €€€

La Pomarada

MAP PAGE 102, POCKET MAP D3
C/Conde Duque 3 Ⓦ lapomarada.es.
Ⓜ Plaza de España.

Café Moderno

Long-standing, no-nonsense Asturian restaurant serving up house speciality *cachopo* (large veal fillets with ham and cheese) in a variety of guises, as well as a good selection of *raciones,* and the – almost obligatory – bottle of cider. €€

El Urogallo

MAP PAGE 102, POCKET MAP A4
Lago de la Casa del Campo Ⓦ elurogallo.es.
Ⓜ Lago.

On the shores of the artificial lake in Casa de Campo, this bar-restaurant has superb views of the Palacio Real and cathedral – perfect for a lazy lunch. Eating a la carte is expensive, but there's a very decent value lunchtime menu. €€€

Tapas bars

Bar Casa Paco

MAP PAGE 102, POCKET MAP A1
C/Altamirano 38 Ⓦ barcasapaco.es.
Ⓜ Argüelles.

Old-style bar close to Parque del Oeste that's been around since the mid-fifties and serves up

some of the best *tortillas* in town, including tasty variations with smoked salmon, goats' cheese, spinach, and steak. €

La Carbonera

MAP PAGE 102, POCKET MAP D2
C/Bernardo López García 11
Ⓦ lacarboneramadrid.com. Ⓜ Plaza de España or Ventura Rodríguez.

Bar/restaurant that specialises in *tablas de queso* (cheese platters), showcasing some of the best Spanish cheese accompanied by wines from small-scale producers. Attentive, knowledgeable service. €€

Txirimiri

MAP PAGE 102, POCKET MAP C7
C/Ferraz 38 Ⓦ txirimiri.es. Ⓜ Argüelles or Ventura Rodríguez.

Branch of an excellent small chain of tapas bars specialising in Basque-style *pintxos* and *raciones*. Favourites include steak with caramelised onion and pepper, smoked sardines with lime mayonnaise, and *chistorra* (sausage) in cider. For something more substantial, the steak, duck and cod are good bets. €€

Live performance at Galileo Galilei

El Jardín Secreto

Bars

Ginkgo

MAP PAGE 102, POCKET MAP C3

Plaza de España 3 ⓦ ginkgoskybarmadrid.com.
Ⓜ Plaza de España.

Modish rooftop cocktail bar located
on the twelfth floor of the *VP
Plaza España* hotel with fantastic
views over the square, but there is
a charge to enter and a dress code
(elegant/casual). Regular live music
and shows (charge).

El Jardín Secreto

MAP PAGE 102, POCKET MAP C2

C/Conde Duque 2 ⓦ eljardinsecretomadrid.es.
Ⓜ Ventura Rodríguez or Plaza de España.

Cosy, dimly-lit bar on the corner
of a tiny plaza close to Plaza de
España serving reasonably priced
drinks and cocktails. Service
is friendly and the atmosphere
unhurried. Also serves food.

Sambhad Cocktail

MAP PAGE 102, POCKET MAP C3

C/Duque de Osuna 4 ⓦ bit.ly/Sambhad.
Ⓜ Plaza de España.

Friendly, unpretentious cocktail
bar with a little terrace perched on
a small plaza above Calle Princesa.
The cocktail menu is extensive,
with over a dozen different types of
mojito and twenty different gins,
and the prices are reasonable too.

La Taberna de Corps

MAP PAGE 102, POCKET MAP C2

Plaza de los Guardia de Corps 1 ☎ 915 475
327. Ⓜ Plaza de España.

The main attraction of this small
corner bar is the terrace just off the
quiet Calle Conde Duque (tables
are hard to come by at weekends).
Good beer and wine, *vermút del
grifo* (vermouth on tap) and an
impressive selection of canapés.

Club

Galileo Galilei

MAP PAGE 102, POCKET MAP C1

C/Galileo 100 ⓦ salagalileogalilei.com.
Ⓜ Islas Filipinas.

Bar, concert venue and disco rolled
into one. Latin music is regularly on
offer, along with cabaret and flamenco.

Day-trips

If you want to take a break from the frenetic activity of the city centre, there are some fascinating day-trips all within easy reach of the Spanish capital. If you only have time for one day-trip, make it Toledo. The city preceded Madrid as the Spanish capital and is today a monument to the many cultures – Visigothic, Moorish, Jewish and Christian – which have shaped the destiny of Spain. Immortalized by El Greco, who lived and worked here for most of his later career, the city is packed with memorable sights. A close second is stunning Segovia, with its spectacular Roman aqueduct, fantasy castle and mountain backdrop. Third on the list is El Escorial, home to Felipe II's vast monastery-palace complex, a monument to out-monument all others, although the adjacent Valle de Cuelgamuros, built under the orders of Franco, is even more megalomaniacal and far more chilling. And not forgetting Aranjuez, an oasis in the parched Castilian plain famed for its strawberries, lavish Baroque palace and gardens, and the plaza at nearby Chinchón, which provides a fabulous setting for a long, lazy lunch.

Toledo cathedral

Visiting Toledo

There are **buses** to Toledo from the bus station in Plaza Elíptica (Ⓜ Plaza Elíptica) in Madrid every thirty minutes, taking about 1hr. The city's bus station is in the modern part of the city; bus #5 runs from it to central Plaza de Zocódover. A high-speed train service from Atocha takes just 30min; it's around €20 for a day return ticket, but purchase this in advance on Ⓦ renfe.com. Toledo's train station is a 20min walk or a bus ride (#5 or #6) from the heart of town. The main **tourist office** (Mon–Fri & Sun 10am–3.30pm, Sat 10am–6pm; Ⓦ turismo.toledo.es) is opposite the cathedral in the Plaza del Consistorio. There's another office (Mon–Sat 8am–4pm, Sun 10am–2pm) at the top of the escalators leading into the city from the Glorieta de La Reconquista, and one outside the city walls opposite the Puerta Nueva de Bisagra (Mon–Sat 10am–6pm, Sun 10am–2pm). You can save on the entry fees to some of the sights if you invest in the *pulsera turística* which is available at many of the key sights (Ⓦ toledomonumental.com).

Toledo

El Alcázar and Museo del Ejército

C/Unión s/n. Tues–Sun 10am–5pm. Charge, free Sun and for under-18's. Ⓦ bit.ly/AlcazarMuseo.

If one building dominates Toledo, it's the imposing fortress of the **Alcázar.** Originally the site of a Roman palace, Emperor Charles V ordered the construction of the current fortress in the sixteenth century, though it has been burned and bombarded so often that little remains of the original building. The monument enjoyed iconic status during the Franco era after the Nationalist forces inside, under siege by the Republican town, were eventually relieved by an army heading for Madrid which took severe retribution on the local inhabitants. After a tortuous relocation and refurbishment programme, the Alcázar is now home to an impressive new army museum. Encompassing a new building constructed over the archeological remains of the original fortress, the museum provides two fascinating routes – one historic and one thematic – through which the role of the Spanish military is examined in exhaustive detail. Exhibits include everything from medieval swords and suits of armour to toy soldiers and Civil War uniforms.

Hospital y Museo de Santa Cruz

C/Cervantes 3. Mon–Sat 10am–6pm, Sun 9am–3pm. Charge, free Wed after 4pm, Sun, and for under-18s. Ⓦ bit.ly/MuseoSC.

A superlative Renaissance building with a magnificent Plateresque main doorway, this refurbished museum houses some of the greatest El Grecos in Toledo, including *The Immaculate Conception* and *The Holy Family*. As well as outstanding works by Luca Giordano and Ribera, there's an impressive collection of exhibits dating from prehistory through to the twentieth century, including archeological finds, ceramics and sculpture.

La Catedral

C/Cardenal Cisneros. Mon–Sat 10am–6pm, Sun 2–6pm. Charge. Ⓦ catedralprimada.es.

Toledo's stunning cathedral reflects the importance of the city that for so long outshone its neighbour, Madrid. A robust Gothic construction, which took over 250 years (1227–1493) to complete,

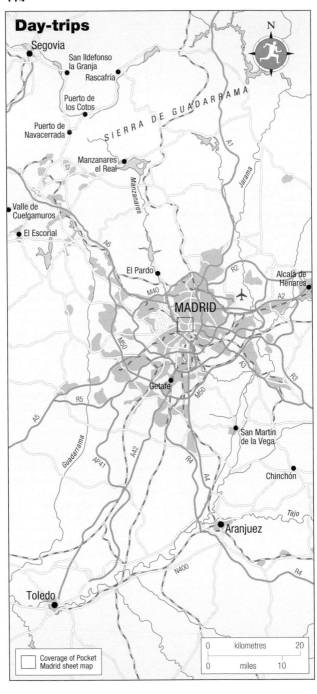

Day-trips

N

Segovia

San Ildefonso
la Granja

Rascafría

Puerto de
los Cotos

SIERRA DE GUADARRAMA

Puerto de
Navacerrada

Manzanares
el Real

Manzanares

Jarama

A1

Valle de
Cuelgamuros

El Escorial

A6

El Pardo

M40

R2

Alcalá de
Henares

A2

MADRID

M50

M50

Getafe

R5

A5

Guadarrama

AP41

A42

R4

A4

R3

San Martín
de la Vega

Chinchón

Tajo

Aranjuez

N400

R4

Toledo

| 0 | kilometres | 20 |
| 0 | miles | 10 |

Coverage of Pocket
Madrid sheet map

it's richly decorated in Gothic, Renaissance and Baroque styles. The cavernous interior is home to some magnificent stained glass, an outstanding **Coro** (Choir), a wonderful **Gothic Capilla Mayor** (Main Chapel) and an extravagant high altar. The cathedral **museums** are worth a look for their impressive collections including paintings by El Greco, Goya and Velázquez, as well as one of El Greco's few surviving pieces of sculpture.

El Alcázar, Toledo

Santo Tomé and the Burial of the Count of Orgaz

Plaza del Conde. Daily: mid–March to mid–Oct 10am–6.45pm; mid–Oct to mid–March 10am–5.45pm. Charge. Ⓦ santotome.org.

Housed alone, in a small annexe of the church of Santo Tomé, one of the most celebrated attractions of Toledo is El Greco's masterpiece, *The Burial of the Count of Orgaz*. The painting depicts the count's funeral, at which St Stephen and St Augustine appeared in order to lower him into the tomb. Combining El Greco's genius for the mystic with his great powers as a portrait painter and master of colour, the work includes a depiction of the artist himself – he can be spotted seventh from the left, looking out at the viewer with his son in the foreground.

Museo del Greco

C/Samuel Levi. March–Oct Tues–Sat 9.30am–7.30pm, Sun 10am–3pm; Nov–Feb Tues–Sat 9.30am–6pm, Sun 10am–3pm. Charge, combined ticket with Museo Sefardi available, free Sat after 2pm, Sun, for under-18s and over-65s. Ⓦ bit.ly/MuseoGreco.

This museum in the former Jewish quarter close to Santo Tomé is devoted to the life and work of the ground-breaking sixteenth-century artist El Greco, so closely associated with Toledo. A refurbished exhibition space houses his famous **View and Map of Toledo**, a series of the Twelve Apostles, completed later than the set in the cathedral, and other outstanding works.

Museo de Victorio Macho

Plaza de Victorio Macho. Mon–Wed & Sun 10am–2pm, Thurs–Sat 11am–6pm. Charge. Ⓦ realfundaciontoledo.es.

Splendidly situated on a spur overlooking the Tajo, this museum contains the sculptures, paintings and sketches of Spanish artist Victorio Macho (1887–1966).

Toledo bars and restaurants

There are plenty of bars and restaurants scattered around the old town, although inevitably most of the options are pretty touristy. For a budget option try *Casa Ludeña* at Plaza Magdalena 13, close to the Alcázar, while *Alfileritos 24* at C/Alferitos 24 offers a creative take on many regional specialities. For more fine dining try *Los Cuatro Tiempos* at C/Sixto Ramón Parro 5.

Visiting Segovia

Segovia is an easy day-trip from Madrid, with up to ten high-speed trains daily (28min) from Atocha and Chamartín stations, plus **buses** leaving from Moncloa bus station (Metro Príncipe Pío; every 30min; 1hr 15min). The high-speed train station is out of town – take bus #11 (every 15min) to the aqueduct. There's a visitor reception centre is situated in the Plaza del Azoguejo (Mon–Fri 10am–2pm & 4–7pm, Sat 10am–7pm, Sun 9am–3pm; ⓦ turismodesegovia.com) by the aqueduct. A regular bus service from Segovia to La Granja operates from the station at Paseo Ezequiel González.

The museum is set in a delightfully tranquil garden with the auditorium on the ground floor showing a documentary film (available in English) about the city and its history.

Museo Sefardí/ Sinagoga del Tránsito

C/Samuel Levi. Tues–Sat 9.30am–6pm (summer until 7.30pm), Sun 10am–3pm. Charge, combined ticket with Museo del Greco available, free Sat after 2pm & Sun. ⓦ bit.ly/MSefardi.

Built along Moorish lines by Samuel Levi in 1366, the Sinagoga del Tránsito became a church after the fifteenth-century expulsion of the Jews and was restored to its original form only in the last century. The interior is a simple galleried hall, brilliantly decorated with polychromed stuccowork and superb filigree windows, while Hebrew inscriptions praising God, King Pedro and Samuel Levi adorn the walls. It also houses a small but engaging Sephardic Museum (same hours) tracing the distinct traditions and development of Jewish culture in Spain.

Sinagoga Santa María la Blanca

C/Reyes Católicos 4. Daily: March to mid-Oct 10am–6.45pm; mid-Oct to Feb 10am–5.45pm. Charge, free under-10s. The second of Toledo's two surviving synagogues, the tranquil Santa María la Blanca pre-dates the Sinagoga del Tránsito by over

a century. Despite having been both a church and synagogue, the horseshoe arches and the fact that it was built by Mudéjar craftsmen give it the look of a mosque. The arches are decorated with elaborate plaster designs of pine cones and palm trees, while its Baroque *retablo* (altarpiece) dates from the time it was a church. The whole effect is stunning, all set off against a deep-red floor that contains some of the original decorative tiles.

Monasterio de San Juan de los Reyes

C/San Juan de los Reyes 2. Daily: March to mid-Oct 10am–6.45pm; mid-Oct to Feb 10am–5.45pm; Charge, free under-10s. The exterior of this beautiful church is bizarrely festooned with the chains worn by Christian prisoners from Granada, who were released on the reconquest of the city in 1492. It was originally a **Franciscan convent** founded by the Reyes Católicos (Catholic Monarchs) Fernando and Isabel – who completed the Christian reconquest of Spain – and in which, until the fall of Granada, they had planned to be buried. Its double-storeyed cloister is outstanding, with an elaborate Mudéjar ceiling in the upper floor.

Convento de Santo Domingo Antiguo

Plaza Santo Domingo Antiguo. Summer: Mon–Sat 11am–1.30pm & 4–7pm, Sun 4–7pm. Charge.

The Convento de Santo Domingo Antiguo's chief claim to fame is as the resting place of El Greco, whose remains lie in the crypt that can be glimpsed through a peephole in the floor. The convent's religious treasures are displayed in the old choir, but more interesting is the high altarpiece of the church – El Greco's first major commission in Toledo. Unfortunately, most of the canvases have gone to museums and are here replaced by copies.

Mezquita del Cristo de la Luz

Cuesta de los Carmelitas Descalzos 10. Daily: March to mid-Oct 10am–6.45pm; mid-Oct to Feb 10am–5.45pm. Charge.

Although this is one of the oldest Moorish monuments in Spain (the mosque was built by Musa Ibn Ali in the tenth century on the foundations of a Visigothic church), only the nave, with its nine different cupolas, is the original Arab construction. The apse was added when the building was converted into a church, and is claimed to be the first product of the Mudéjar style. The mosque itself, set in a tiny patio-like park and open on all sides to the elements, is so small that it seems more like a miniature summer pavilion, but it has an elegant simplicity of design that few of the town's great monuments can match.

Segovia

The Aqueduct

Plaza del Azoguejo.

Over 700m long and almost 30m high, Segovia's aqueduct is an impressive sight. Built without a drop of mortar or cement, it has been here since around the end of the first century AD – no one knows exactly when – though it no longer carries water to the city. For an excellent view of both the aqueduct and the city, climb the stairs beside it up to a surviving fragment of the city walls.

La Catedral

Plaza Mayor. Daily: April–Oct 9am–9.30pm; Nov–March 9.30am–6.30pm. Charge, free on Sun: April–Oct 9–10am, Nov–March 9.30–10.30am, and for under-8s. Ⓦ catedralsegovia.es.

Segovia cathedral

Segovia's cathedral was the last major Gothic building constructed in Spain. Pinnacles and flying buttresses are tacked on at every conceivable point, although the interior is surprisingly bare and its space is cramped by a great green marble choir in the very centre. The cathedral's treasures are almost all confined to the museum (same hours).

The Alcázar

Plaza Reina Victoria Eugenia. Daily: April–Oct 10am–8pm; Nov–March 10am–6pm. Charge. Ⓦ alcazardesegovia.com.

At the edge of town and overlooking the valley of the Eresma river is the Alcázar, an extraordinary fantasy of a castle with its narrow towers and flurry of turrets. Although it dates from the fourteenth and fifteenth centuries, it was almost completely destroyed by a fire in 1862 and rebuilt as a deliberately exaggerated version of the original. Inside, the rooms are decked out with armour, weapons and tapestries, but the major attractions are the splendid wooden sculptured ceilings and the magnificent panoramas.

Vera Cruz

Carretera Zamarramala. Tues 4–6pm, Wed–Sun 10.30am–1.30pm & 4–6pm. Closed Nov. Charge, free Wed pm.

This remarkable twelve-sided church stands in the valley facing the Alcázar. Built by the Knights Templar in the early thirteenth century on the pattern of the Church of the Holy Sepulchre in Jerusalem, it once housed part of the supposed True Cross (hence its name). Today, you can climb the tower for a highly photogenic view of the city, while nearby is a very pleasant riverside walk along the banks of the tranquil Eresma river.

Convento de San Antonio el Real

C/San Antonio el Real Tues–Sat 10am–2pm & 4–6.30pm, Sun 10.45am–2pm. Charge.

If you follow the line of the aqueduct away from the old city for about ten minutes, you will come to a little gem of a palace originally founded by Enrique IV in 1455 and containing an intriguing collection of Mudéjar and Hispano-Flemish art. The convent, part of which now serves as a luxury hotel, has some of the most beautiful **artesonado** (wooden sculptured) ceilings in the city and there's a wonderfully detailed fifteenth-century wooden Calvary in the main church.

La Granja

Gardens daily: 10am–dusk. Palace daily: April–Sept 10am–8pm; Oct–March 10am–6pm. Charge, free Wed & Sun: April–Sept 3–7pm; Oct–March 3–6pm. Ⓦ patrimonionacional.es.

The summer palace of La Granja was built by the first Bourbon king of Spain, Felipe V, no doubt in another attempt to alleviate his homesickness for Versailles. Its chief appeal lies in its mountain setting and extravagant wooded grounds and gardens, but it's also worth casting an eye over the plush furnishings and fabulous tapestries of the palace which, though damaged by a fire in 1918, has been successfully restored.

Segovia restaurants

Segovia is renowned for its delicious Castilian roasts; some of the best places to sample the local specialities are the *Mesón José María* at C/Cronista Lecea 11, just off the Plaza Mayor, *Mesón de Cándido* below the aqueduct at Plaza del Azoguejo 5 and *Casa Duque* at nearby C/Cervantes 12.

Visiting El Escorial

There are around 25 **trains** a day to El Escorial from Madrid (5.45am–11.30pm from Atocha, calling at Chamartín), or **buses** (#661 and #664 from the intercambiador at Moncloa) run every fifteen minutes on weekdays and hourly at weekends. The tourist office is at C/Grimaldi 4 (Mon–Sat 10am–2pm & 3–6pm, Sun 10am–2pm, ⓦ sanlorenzoturismo.es) just north of the visitors' entrance to the monastery. To visit the Valle de Cuelgamuros from El Escorial, take a local bus (#660), which starts from the bus station at C/Juan de Toledo 3.

Outside, the highlight of the eighteenth-century gardens is a series of majestic fountains. They're a fantastic spectacle, with some of the jets rising 40 metres, but they usually only operate between Easter and July – at 1pm on Sundays and 5.30pm on Wednesdays and Saturdays – with special displays on May 30, July 25 and August 25 (charge, check website for details).

El Escorial

El Escorial and Valle de Cuelgamuros

El Escorial

Tues–Sun: 10am–7pm. Charge; free Wed & Sun: 5–7pm. ⓦ patrimonionacional.es.
El Escorial was the largest Spanish building of the Renaissance, built to celebrate a victory over the French in

El Escorial

1557 and divided into different
sections for secular and religious
use. Linking the two zones is the
Biblioteca (Library), a splendid
hall with vivid, multicoloured
frescoes by Tibaldi, and
containing some gorgeously
executed Arabic manuscripts.

The enormous, cold, dark
interior of the Basílica contains
over forty altars, designed to allow
simultaneous Masses to be held.
Behind the main altar lies some
of Felipe II's mammoth collection
of saintly relics, including six
whole bodies, over sixty heads and
hundreds of bone fragments set in
fabulously expensive caskets.

Many of the monastery's religious
treasures are contained in the
Sacristía and Salas Capitulares
and include paintings by Titian,
Velázquez and José Ribera. Below
these rooms is the Panteón Real,
where past Spanish monarchs lie in
their gilded marble tombs. The royal
children are laid in the Panteón de
los Infantes and there's also a babies'
tomb with room for sixty infants.

What remains of El Escorial's art
collection – works by Bosch, Dürer,
Titian, Zurbarán, among others that
escaped transfer to the Prado – is
kept in the elegant Museos Nuevos.
Don't miss the Sala de Batallas, a
long gallery lined with an epic series

El Escorial's ornate library

Visiting Aranjuez and Chinchón

From the end of April to July and September to mid-October, a weekend service on an old wooden steam train, the **Tren de la Fresa**, runs between Madrid and Aranjuez. It leaves the Príncipe Pío around 10am and departs from Aranjuez at 7pm (⬥ trendelafresa.es). The fare includes a guided bus tour in Aranjuez, entry to the monuments and *fresas con nata* (strawberries and cream) on the train. Standard trains leave every 15–30min from Atocha, with the last train returning from Aranjuez at about 11.30pm. **Buses** run every half-hour during the week and every hour at weekends from Estación Sur. You'll find a helpful **tourist office** in the Casa de Infantes (Mon–Fri 10am–2pm & 4–6pm, Sat & Sun 10am–6pm; ⬥ visita.aranjuez. es & ⬥ aranjuez.com).There are hourly buses (#337) from Madrid **to Chinchón** from the bus station at Avda Mediterráneo 49 near the Plaza Conde Casal, or you can reach the town from Aranjuez on the service from Avenida de las Infantas (Mon–Fri hourly, Sat & Sun 8 daily; #430). There's a small **tourist office** in the Plaza Mayor (daily 10am–2pm & 4–6pm, ⬥ ciudad-chinchon.com).

For a classic Castilian lunch in Chinchón, try the *Mesón el Comendador, La Casa del Pregonero* or *La Balconada* overlooking the main plaza or the nearby *Mesón Cuevas del Vino*.

of paintings depicting important imperial battles. Finally, there are the treasure-crammed Salones Reales (Royal Apartments), containing the austere quarters of Felipe II, with the chair that supported his gouty leg and the deathbed from which he was able to contemplate the high altar of the Basílica.

La Silla de Felipe

Around 3km out of town is the Silla de Felipe – "Felipe's Seat" – a chair carved into a rocky outcrop with a great view of the palace, and from where the king is supposed to have watched the building's construction. You can reach it on foot by following the path which starts by the arches beyond the main entrance to the Biblioteca; keep to the left as you go down the hill and then cross the main road and follow the signs. If you have a car, take the M 505 Ávila road and turn off at the sign after about 3km.

Valle de Cuelgamuros

Tues–Sun: 10am–7pm. Charge; free Wed & Sun: 3–7pm. ⬥ patrimonionacional.es.

Formerly known as the Valle de los Caídos (valley of the fallen), this bleak basilica complex, with its giant 150m-high cross, was constructed by Franco to honour his victory over the democratically elected government of the Second Republic in the Spanish Civil War. The grim, pompous architectural forms employed, the constant inscriptions "Fallen for God and for Spain" and the proximity to El Escorial clue you in to its other function – the glorification of General Franco and his regime.

The socialist government of Pedro Sánchez tried to convert the site into a place of memorial for all the victims of the Civil War by beginning work to exhume and re-bury the bodies of the Republican prisoners who were forced to build the complex. After much legal wrangling it also finally managed to remove the remains of Franco and that of his guru, the Falangist leader, José Antonio Primo de Rivera who had been buried in tombs within the basilica.

Aranjuez and Chinchón restaurants

El Rana Verde (ⓦ elranaverde.com), close to the palace and on the banks of the river at Plaza Santiago Rusiñol, is probably Aranjuez's best-known restaurant, and serves a selection of set menus.

Aranjuez and Chinchón

The Palacio Real

April–Sept Mon–Sat 10am–7pm, Sun 10am–4pm, Oct–March Mon–Sat 10am–6pm, Sun 10am–4pm. Charge. ⓦ patrimonionacional.es.

The present building dates from the 1700s and was an attempt by Spain's Bourbon monarchs to create a Spanish Versailles. The palace is noted for its exotic decor highlighted in the fabulously elaborate Porcelain and Smoking rooms.

Jardín de la Isla and Jardín del Príncipe

Daily 8.30am–dusk. Free.

Two palace gardens worthy of a visit are the Jardín de la Isla with its fountains and neatly tended gardens, and the more attractive Jardín del Príncipe, which inspired Rodrigo's famous *Concierto de Aranjuez*, offering shaded walks along the river and plenty of spots for a siesta.

Casa del Labrador

Jardín del Príncipe. Tues–Sun 10am–7pm. Charge.

At the far end of the Jardín del Príncipe is the Casa del Labrador

Peacock in the gardens of the Palacio Real

The Palacio Real, Aranjuez

(Peasant's House), which is anything but what its name implies. The house contains more silk, marble, crystal and gold than would seem possible to cram into so small a place, as well as a huge collection of fancy clocks. Although the hotchpotch of styles will offend purists, this miniature palace still provides a fascinating insight into the tastes of the Bourbon dynasty.

Casa de los Marinos (Falúas Reales)

Tues–Sun 10am–7pm. Charge, included with entrance to Palacio Real.

The small Casa de los Marinos museum contains the brightly coloured launches in which royalty would take to the river – try the modern equivalent with a 45-minute boat trip through the royal parks from the jetty by the bridge next to the palace (Sat & Sun 12.30 & 5.30pm; Ⓦ elcuriosity.com; charge).

Plaza de Toros

Guided tours via Ⓦ bit.ly/PlazaToros.

Aranjuez's beautiful eighteenth-century Plaza de Toros houses an exhibition space, part of which is made up of a **bullfighting museum**, while the rest traces the town's history and royal heritage. Nearby, on C/Naranja and C/Rosa, there are a number of *corrales*, traditional-style wooden-balconied tenement blocks.

Chinchón

A stroll around the elegant little town of Chinchón, followed by lunch at one of its restaurants, is a popular pastime for *madrileños*. Noteworthy monuments include a fifteenth-century castle (not open to visitors), a picture-postcard medieval Plaza Mayor and the Iglesia de la Asunción, with a panel by Goya of *The Assumption of the Virgin*, but it is as the home of *anís* that the town is best known. To sample the local aniseed spirit, try one of the local bars or the Alcoholera de Chinchón, a shop on the Plaza Mayor – most visitors come for a tasting before eating at one of the town's traditional *mesones*.

ACCOMMODATION

Palace Hotel

Accommodation

Madrid has a plentiful supply of accommodation and most of it is very central. With increasing competition in the sector, many hotels have been busy upgrading facilities in recent years and there is now a much wider range of stylish, medium-priced hotels, including more design-conscious boutique hotels. The city has a growing number of exclusive top-range hotels too, while if you're after a budget place to stay, go for one of the hostales – small, frequently family-run establishments housed in large, centrally located apartment blocks. The main factor to consider in choosing a place is location. To be at the heart of the old town, choose the areas around Puerta del Sol, Plaza de Santa Ana or Plaza Mayor; for nightlife, Malasaña or Chueca will appeal; if you are looking for a quieter location and a bit more luxury, consider the Paseo del Prado, Recoletos or Salamanca areas; and if you are with children the areas by the main parks are good options. Another thing to bear in mind is noise. Madrid is a high-decibel city so avoid rooms on lower floors or choose a place away from the action. As for facilities, wi-fi is standard as is air conditioning, a welcome extra in summer. The price codes reflect the cost of a double room during high season.

Madrid de los Austrias

HOSTAL LA MACARENA MAP PAGE 28, POCKET MAP B13. C/Cava de San Miguel 8, 2° Ⓦ silserranos.com. Ⓜ Sol. Family-run *hostal* in a back street just beside Plaza Mayor. The twelve neat, well-kept rooms are on the small side, but all have bathroom and satellite TV. It can be a little noisy, but the location is perfect. €

Booking accommodation

Madrid's increasing popularity as a weekend-break destination means that it's best to book accommodation in advance if possible. Nearly all hotels will have website reservation facilities and nearly all understand English.

Hotels in the more expensive categories run special weekend offers, so it's always worth checking their websites for details. Good deals and the lowest prices are usually available in the summer months, but it is best to avoid Spanish national holidays, when prices peak.

If you do arrive without a reservation, the tourist information service at the airport, train and bus stations can usually help (branches and contact details are under Tourist Information in the Directory section; see page 143).

Accommodation price codes

All the accommodation detailed in this Guide has been graded according to the four price categories listed below. These represent how much you can expect to pay in each establishment for a standard double or twin room in high season barring special deals and discounts; for a single room, expect to pay around eighty percent of the price of a double. Our categories are simply a guide to prices and do not give an indication of the facilities you might expect; as such they differ from the star-system applied by the tourist authorities.

€	up to €100
€€	€101–150
€€€	€151–220
€€€€	€220 and above

HOSTAL MADRID MAP PAGE 28, POCKET MAP D12. C/Esparteros 6 ⓦ hostal-madrid. info. Ⓜ Sol. In a fantastic setting between Sol and Plaza Mayor, this no frills *hostal* is renowned for its clean, modern, en-suite rooms and friendly service. Rooms can be a little noisy, but this is more than compensated for by the location. Triples and quadruples available. €

HOTEL MAYERLING MAP PAGE 28, POCKET MAP D13. C/Conde de Romanones 6 ⓦ mayerlinghotel.com. Ⓜ Tirso de Molina. This stylish, designer hotel is housed in a former textile warehouse close to Calle de Atocha. Clean lines and black and white decor predominate in the simple, neat, sound-proofed rooms. There's a sun terrace and free tea and coffee in the lobby. €€

HOTEL THE HAT MAP PAGE 28, POCKET MAP C13. C/Imperial 9 ⓦ thehatmadrid. com. Ⓜ La Latina. Modern, centrally located hostel with hotel-like services and a wonderful roof-top bar. A range of accommodation available from dormitories and family rooms to female-only doubles and suites. All the pine-furnished rooms are bright and airy, some have private bathrooms. There is a good buffet breakfast. €

PESTANA PLAZA MAYOR MAP PAGE 28, POCKET MAP C13. C/Imperial 8 ⓦ pestanacollection.com. Ⓜ Sol or Tirso de Molina. Overlooking the bustling Plaza Mayor, this luxury hotel has a spa, indoor patio area, rooftop bar and pool with great views over the centre of town. The more expensive rooms look out on the plaza. €€€

PETIT PALACE POSADA DEL PEINE MAP PAGE 28, POCKET MAP C12. C/Postas 17 ⓦ petitpalaceposadadelpeine.com. Ⓜ Sol. This upmarket branch of the *Petit Palace* hotel chain is situated in a refurbished building right next to the Plaza Mayor and was once the site of a seventeenth-century inn. Sleek rooms with minimalist decor and stylish fittings. Family rooms also available. Buffet and free use of bicycles to tour the city centre. €€€

POSADA DEL DRAGÓN MAP PAGE 28, POCKET MAP B14. C/Cava Baja 14 ⓦ posadadeldragon.com. Ⓜ La Latina. Slap back in the middle of one of the best streets for tapas in Madrid, this historic inn has been refurbished and turned into a boutique hotel. Compact, brightly-coloured, themed rooms with comfortable beds and flat-screen TVs. Very popular bar-restaurant downstairs, serving up tasty *raciones*. €€€

POSADA DEL LEÓN DE ORO MAP PAGE 28, POCKET MAP B14. C/Cava Baja 12 ⓦ posadadelleondeoro.com. Ⓜ La Latina. This former inn has been converted into a chic, designer hotel with 17 large, individually decorated rooms complete with walk-in showers and flat-screen TVs. Three-night minimum stay at some times of year. Family rooms and a penthouse also on offer. Good breakfasts and a very good bar restaurant. €€€

Ópera

HOSTAL CENTRAL PALACE MAP PAGE 38, POCKET MAP A11. Plaza de Oriente 2, 3° Ⓦ centralpalacemadrid.com. Ⓜ Ópera. Smartly furnished and very friendly *hostal* with a fabulous location on the plaza. All of the airy rooms are en-suite and well equipped, and some have views over the plaza towards the Palacio Real. €€

HOSTAL DON ALFONSO MAP PAGE 38, POCKET MAP C11. Plaza Celenque 1, 2° Ⓦ hostaldonalfonso.es. Ⓜ Sol. Just off the pedestrianized shopping street C/Arenal and a stone's throw from Sol, this clean, recently refurbished, family-owned *hostal* has fourteen doubles, two triples and some singles, all with bathrooms, a/c and TV. €

HOTEL FRANCISCO I MAP PAGE 38, POCKET MAP C11. C/Arenal 15 Ⓦ hotelfrancisco.com. Ⓜ Ópera. Located close to the opera house, this recently refitted hotel has smart, minimalist rooms, including family options and a terrace suite. Free breakfast with web bookings. €€

HOSTAL GALA MAP PAGE 38, POCKET MAP B10. C/Costanilla de los Ángeles 15 Ⓦ hostalgala.com. Ⓜ Callao. An upmarket, very tasteful *hostal* close to the shopping areas of C/Preciados and Gran Vía. All the modern rooms have power showers and flat-screen TVs. Some have small balconies and there are family rooms available. €€

HOSTAL ORIENTE MAP PAGE 38, POCKET MAP B11. C/Arenal 23 Ⓦ hostaloriente. es. Ⓜ Ópera. Well-appointed, friendly and professional *hostal* close to the opera house. The nineteen refitted en-suite rooms are comfortable and some have views over the plaza. €

HOTEL MENINAS MAP PAGE 38, POCKET MAP B10. C/Campomanes 7 Ⓦ hotelmeninas.es. Ⓜ Ópera. A stylish 37-room hotel in a quiet street near the Teatro Real. Professional staff, fantastic attic rooms and flat-screen TVs. Guests can use the gym and sauna at the nearby *Hotel Ópera*. Breakfast included for web reservations. €€€

OCEAN DRIVE MADRID MAP PAGE 38, POCKET MAP B11. Plaza Isabel II Ⓦ od-hotels.com. Ⓜ Ópera. Opposite the opera house, this new hotel has 72 airy, comfortable rooms, a rooftop terrace with a bar and pool. The deluxe rooms have views over the plaza. €€€

HOTEL PALACIO DE SAN MARTÍN MAP PAGE 38, POCKET MAP C10. Plaza de San Martín 5 Ⓦ intur.com. Ⓜ Ópera. Situated in an attractive square by the Descalzas Reales monastery, this elegant, old-school hotel offers spacious rooms, a small gym and sauna, plus a rooftop restaurant. €€

PETIT PALACE ARENAL MAP PAGE 38, POCKET MAP C11. C/Arenal 16 Ⓦ petitpalacearenal.com. Ⓜ Sol. A member of a popular hotel chain with 64 sleek, snug, modern rooms. There are special family and multi-bed rooms too, though the location can be a little noisy. Another member of the chain, the *Puerta del Sol*, is close by at C/Arenal 4. €€€

ROOM MATE MARIO MAP PAGE 38, POCKET MAP B10. C/Campomanes 4 Ⓦ room-matehotels.com. Ⓜ Ópera. Hip designer hotel close to the Teatro Real. Staff are friendly and the ultra-cool rooms, though compact, are well equipped with neat bathrooms and flat-screen TVs. €€

Our picks

Friendly – *Hostal Gonzalo* see page 130
Good value – *Hostal Gala* see page 128
Boutique – *Room Mate Mario* see page 128
Designer chic – *Hotel Urban* see page 130
Location – *Hostal Central Palace* see page 128
Exclusive – *Hotel Orfila* see page 132
Family – *Hotel Indigo* see page 133

Rastro, Lavapíes and Embajadores

HOTEL ARTRIP MAP PAGE 46, POCKET MAP F9. C/Valencia 11 Ⓦ artriphotel. com. Ⓜ lavapiés. This self-styled "Art Hotel" is conveniently located close to the Reina Sofia and other art galleries. It has seventeen sleek, design-conscious rooms, including family options, that combine the modern with the traditional. Buffet breakfast included in website bookings. €€

HOSTAL BARRERA MAP PAGE 46, POCKET MAP G7. C/Atocha 96, 2° Ⓦ hostalbarrera.com. Ⓜ Antón Martín. Upmarket fourteen-room *hostal* a short distance from Atocha station and with an English-speaking owner. The smart rooms are a cut above most found in this category and the bathrooms are modern. One of the better ones in this part of town. €

CATS HOSTEL MAP PAGE 46, POCKET MAP E14. C/Cañizares 6 Ⓦ catshostels. com. Ⓜ Tirso de Molina. Lively hostel which specialzses in group bookings. It has a bar, an Andalucian-style courtyard patio and a cellar space which acts as a club at night. Doubles and single-sex rooms are available, otherwise accommodation is in clean, a/c dorms for between six to 12 people. €

HOTEL PORCEL GANIVET MAP PAGE 46, POCKET MAP C8. C/Toledo 111–113 Ⓦ hotelganivet.com. Ⓜ Puerta de Toledo. Comfortable, business-style hotel with a rooftop jacuzzi and sun terrace situated at the quieter end of this street. Some of the more expensive rooms have small balconies. €€

TRYP ATOCHA MAP PAGE 46, POCKET MAP G14. C/Atocha 83 Ⓦ melia.com. Ⓜ Antón Martín. This large, business-style hotel, which is not far from Huertas, has modern rooms with all the facilities you'd expect, though some are a little small. Family rooms with bunks for children too. €€€

Sol, Santa Ana and Huertas

HOSTAL ALASKA MAP PAGE 52, POCKET MAP E12. C/Espoz y Mina 7, 4° dcha Ⓦ hostalalaska.es. Ⓜ Sol. Doubles, triples and a single in this modest, but friendly *hostal*. All seven of the basic, brightly decorated rooms have bathrooms and TV. €€

HOSTAL ARMESTO MAP PAGE 52, POCKET MAP G13. C/San Agustín 6, 1° dcha Ⓦ hostalarmesto.com. Ⓜ Antón Martín. Charming eight-room *hostal* in the centre of the city. The pleasantly decorated rooms all have small bathrooms and TV. The best ones overlook the delightful little garden in the Casa de Lope de Vega next door. Very well positioned for the Huertas/Santa Ana area. €€

B&B HOTEL MADRID CENTRO PUERTA DEL SOL MAP PAGE 52, POCKET MAP E11. C/Montera 10–12 Ⓦ hotel-bb.es. Ⓜ Sol. A great location for this friendly, modern hotel with comfortable, functional rooms, some with small terraces. Breakfast is included, with coffee, tea and fruit available all day. €€

CATALONIA PLAZA MAYOR MAP PAGE 52, POCKET MAP E13. C/Atocha 35 Ⓦ cataloniahotels.com. Ⓜ Antón Martín. Close to Plaza Santa Ana and the Huertas area, this modern business-style hotel has spacious, functional rooms with slick modern decor and comfortable beds. There's a small fitness area and jacuzzi as well. €€€

ME MADRID REINA VICTORIA MAP PAGE 52, POCKET MAP E13. Plaza de Santa Ana 14 Ⓦ melia.com. Ⓜ Sol. Once a favourite haunt of bullfighters, this giant white wedding cake of a hotel that dominates the plaza is now part of the exclusive *ME* chain. It comes complete with the de rigueur minimalist decor, designer furnishings, high-tech fittings, a super cool penthouse bar and a very good tapas bar in the foyer. €€€€

ONE SHOT PRADO 23 MAP PAGE 52, POCKET MAP G12. C/Prado 23 Ⓦ hoteloneshotprado23.com. Ⓜ Sevilla or Antón Martín. Smart, minimalist, recent arrival situated in the thick of things in Huertas. A range of room options available from the basic "Económica" to the more spacious

"Ejecutiva", but all are bright with sleek furnishings, walk-in showers and comfortable beds. €€

PETIT PALACE PUERTA DEL SOL MAP PAGE 52, POCKET MAP D11. C/Arenal 4 Ⓦ petitpalacepuertadelsol.com. Ⓜ Sol. One of a chain of hotels that offer good rates and decent services. This one is in a refurbished mansion close to Sol and has the trademark smart, well-appointed rooms with a range of facilities. €€€

HOSTAL PERSAL MAP PAGE 52, POCKET MAP E13. Plaza del Angel 12 Ⓦ hostalpersal.com. Ⓜ Sol. Eighty-room *hostal* close to Plaza Santa Ana that's closer to a hotel in terms of services and facilities. The simple, clean rooms all have bathrooms and TVs. Triples and quadruples available too. €€

ROOM MATE ALICIA MAP PAGE 52, POCKET MAP F13. C/Prado 2 Ⓦ room-matehotels.com. Ⓜ Sol. Perched on the corner of Plaza Santa Ana, *Alicia* is in a great location, if a little noisy. Seriously cool decor by interior designer Pascua Ortega, stylish rooms and unbeatable value. There are suites with great views over the plaza, one of which has a small plunge pool. €€€

HOTEL URBAN MAP PAGE 52, POCKET MAP G12. C/San Jerónimo 34 Ⓦ hotelurban.com. Ⓜ Sevilla. Über cool, fashion-conscious, five-star hotel in the heart of town. The designer rooms come with all mod cons, a rooftop pool, a summer terrace and two "pijo" cocktail bars. It even has its own small museum consisting of items from owner Jordi Clos's collection of Egyptian and Chinese art. Look out for special deals on the website. €€€€

HOTEL VINCCI SOHO MAP PAGE 52, POCKET MAP G13. C/Prado 18 Ⓦ vinccisoho.com. Ⓜ Antón Martín. A great location in the heart of Huertas for this four-star 170-room hotel. Smart wooden decor and furnishings and modern facilities, though bathrooms are rather small. Worth it only if you can get one of the cheaper offers online. €€€

Paseo del Arte and Retiro

HOSTAL GONZALO MAP PAGE 66, POCKET MAP H13. C/Cervantes 34, 3° Ⓦ hostalgonzalo.com. Ⓜ Antón Martín. One of the most welcoming *hostales* in the city, tucked away close to Paseo del Prado. Fifteen simple, bright, en-suite rooms, all of which have TVs and refurbished bathrooms. It's a very good-value, smart place run by charming owner Antonio and his brother Javier. €

MANDARIN ORIENTAL RITZ MAP PAGE 66, POCKET MAP J12. Plaza de la Lealtad 5 Ⓦ mandarinoriental.com. Ⓜ Banco de España. Reopened after lengthy restoration of the belle epoque mansion in which it is located, the Ritz has all the no-holds-barred luxury and exclusivity you would expect of a hotel that bears its name, plus a perfect location close to the Prado. €€€€

MERCURE MADRID CENTRO MAP PAGE 66, POCKET MAP H13. C/Lope de Vega 49 Ⓦ accorhotels.com. Ⓜ Estación del Arte. With a great location close to the main art galleries, this hotel is a good mid-priced option. The business-style rooms are neat and comfortable. €€

NH PASEO DEL PRADO MAP PAGE 66, POCKET MAP H13. Plaza Cánovas del Castillo 4 Ⓦ nh-hotels.com. Ⓜ Banco de España. This large, plush member of the *NH Collection* chain is attractively situated in front of the Neptune fountain on the Paseo del Prado. Excellent facilities and a perfect location for the nearby art galleries. The hotel's restaurant serves some high-class tapas too. There is a slightly cheaper sister hotel, the *NH Nacional*, just up the road at Paseo del Prado 48. €€€

NUMA SCRIPT MAP PAGE 66, POCKET MAP H12. Plaza de los Cortes 4 Ⓦ numastays.com. Ⓜ Banco de España. Stripped down, quite small, modern rooms in this well-located option near the Congreso. No reception service and contactless check-in, but if you are just looking for a good-value room, this is a nice option. €

ONE SHOT RECOLETOS 04 MAP PAGE 66, POCKET MAP J4. C/Salustiano Olózaga 4 Ⓦ hoteloneshotrecoletos04. com. Ⓜ Retiro. A great location close to the Retiro and in the midst of the refined streets of the Recoletos area, this modern hotel has 42 wooden-floored rooms with comfortable beds, small but neat bathrooms and sound-proofed windows. There are budget, standard and premium options available. €€

HOTEL PALACE MAP PAGE 66, POCKET MAP H12–13. Plaza de las Cortes 7 Ⓦ westinpalacemadrid.com. Ⓜ Sol or Sevilla. Colossal, sumptuous hotel with every imaginable facility, but none of the snootiness you might expect from its aristocratic appearance. A spectacular, glass-covered central patio and luxurious rooms are part of its charm. €€€€

RADISSON BLU, MADRID PRADO MAP PAGE 66, POCKET MAP J14. C/ Moratín 52, Plaza de Platería Martínez Ⓦ radissonblu.com. Ⓜ Estación del Arte. Designer hotel located along the Paseo del Prado featuring sleek rooms in black, brown and white, photos of the Madrid skyline adorning the walls, black slate bathrooms and coffee machines. There is a small spa area and indoor pool, a decent bar and a restaurant too. €€€

URBAN SEA ATOCHA 113 MAP PAGE 66, POCKET MAP G7. C/Atocha 113, 3° Ⓦ blueseahotels.com. Ⓜ Estación del Arte. Just across the roundabout from Atocha station, this member of the *Blue Sea* chain contains 36 simple, clean-lined rooms at a very competitive price. A sun terrace on the sixth floor and the location make it a good option. €€

HOTEL VILLA REAL MAP PAGE 66, POCKET MAP G12. Plaza de las Cortes 10 Ⓦ hotelvillareal.com. Ⓜ Sol. Aristocratic and highly original, the *Villa Real* comes complete with its own art collection owned by Catalan entrepreneur Jordi Clos. Each of the elegant double rooms has a spacious sitting area (there are several suites too) and many have a balcony overlooking the plaza. The New York-style *East 47* restaurant, which has some Andy Warhol

originals on the wall, serves up quality tapas, while there is a small pool on the rooftop terrace. €€€

HOTEL VINCCI SOMA MAP PAGE 66, POCKET MAP K3. C/Goya 79 Ⓦ vinccisoma.com. Ⓜ Goya. This bright, modern hotel, which is close to the Salamanca shops and Plaza Colón, has a sophisticated feel to it with its tasteful rooms and good service. €€€

VP JARDÍN DE RECOLETOS MAP PAGE 66, POCKET MAP J4. C/Gil de Santivañes 6 Ⓦ recoletos-hotel.com. Ⓜ Retiro or Serrano. If you are looking for a little peace and quiet, this elegant four-star hotel close to the Retiro is a very good option. The 43 recently refurbished rooms are spacious and well furnished, while the real attraction is the lovely shady garden terrace. The price is very competitive too. €€€

Gran Vía, Chueca and Malasaña

B&B HOTEL MADRID CENTRO FUENCARRAL 52 MAP PAGE 80, POCKET MAP F3. C/Fuencarral 52 Ⓦ hotel-bb.es. Ⓜ Chueca or Tribunal. Opened on the site of a former *hostal* in 2015, this mid-range option is right on a fashionable, pedestrianized shopping street in the heart of Chueca. Minimalist decor, modern bathrooms with walk-in showers and large beds. €€

IBEROSTAR LAS LETRAS GRAN VÍA MAP PAGE 80, POCKET MAP F10. Gran Vía 11 Ⓦ iberostar.com. Ⓜ Gran Vía. An elegant, design-conscious hotel housed in a lovely early nineteenth-century building at the smarter end of Gran Vía. The stylish, high-ceilinged rooms decorated with literary quotations come complete with plasma TVs. Downstairs, there's a smooth bar and lounge area, and a high-quality restaurant with reasonably priced dishes. Look out for offers on the website. €€€€

ONLY YOU BOUTIQUE HOTEL MAP PAGE 80, POCKET MAP G4. C/Barquillo

21 ⓦ onlyyouhotels.com. Ⓜ Chueca. A relatively new arrival on the scene, this boutique-style hotel, housed in a refurbished nineteenth-century building, is in a great location between Chueca and Recoletos. There are seventy chic, individually decorated rooms, plus a gastro-bar, a cocktail lounge and a small gym. €€€€

PETIT PALACE CHUECA MAP PAGE 80, POCKET MAP F4. C/Hortaleza 3 ⓦ petitpalacechueca.com. Ⓜ Gran Vía. A former *hostal* upgraded and refurbished to become one of the *Petit Palace* chain of hotels. Situated in the heart of Chueca, it has 58 neat rooms, including larger family options with bunk beds. €€

ROOM MATE ÓSCAR MAP PAGE 80, POCKET MAP F4. Plaza Pedro Zerolo12 ⓦ room-matehotels.com. Ⓜ Gran Vía. Part of the hip *Room Mate* chain, the *Óscar* is in the heart of Chueca and popular with the gay community. It has a garish psychedelic lobby, super cool sparkling white bar area, as well as space age, design-conscious rooms and a rooftop splash pool (additional charge) popular for evening cocktails. €€€

HOSTAL SIL/SERRANOS MAP PAGE 80, POCKET MAP f2. C/Fuencarral 95, 2° & 3° ⓦ silserranos.com. Ⓜ Tribunal. Two friendly *hostales* located at the quieter end of C/Fuencarral in Malasaña. A variety of simple but comfortable rooms all with modern bathrooms and TV. Triples and quadruples available. €

HOTEL PRINCIPAL MAP PAGE 80, POCKET MAP H10. C/Marqués de Valdeiglesias 1 ⓦ theprincipalmadrid hotel.com. Ⓜ Banco de España. Luxury five-star hotel with large, modern rooms with walk-in showers, a seventh-floor roof-top cocktail bar with wonderful views across Gran Vía and an attic restaurant run by Michelin-star chef Ramón Freixa. €€€€

HOTEL URSO MAP PAGE 80, POCKET MAP F2. C/Mejía Lequerica 8 ⓦ hotelurso. com. Ⓜ Alonso Martínez. An upmarket hotel sandwiched between Chamberí and Chueca. Rooms are spacious – most have

a small sitting area – well equipped and comfortable. There is a small spa area and a pleasant bar and bamboo-fringed indoor terrace. €€€€

VINCCI THE MINT MAP PAGE 80, POCKET MAP F4. Gran Vía 10 ⓦ vinccithemint. com. Ⓜ Gran Vía. A new, luxury, designer hotel housed in a characterful mansion on Gran Vía. Stylish vintage decor by Jaime Beristain and a range of cool. comfortable rooms available from doubles to suites with a roof-top terrace. €€€€

HOSTAL ZAMORA MAP PAGE 80, POCKET MAP F4. Plaza Pedro Zerolo 1, 4° izda ⓦ hostalzamora.com. Ⓜ Gran Vía. Seventeen simple, clean rooms in an agreeable family-run place, most of which overlook the plaza. All rooms have modern bathrooms and TV. There are good-value family rooms too. Closed August. €

Salamanca and Paseo de la Castellana

ICON EMBASSY MAP PAGE 92, POCKET MAP J2. C/Serrano 46 ⓦ iconembassy.com. Ⓜ Serrano. Given a head-to-toe make-over in 2018, this hotel is close to Plaza Colón and in the middle of the upmarket Salamanca shopping district. The *Embassy* has 75 minimalist rooms, including family options and a four-person apartment. €€€€

HOTEL ORFILA MAP PAGE 92, POCKET MAP H2. C/Orfila 6 ⓦ hotelorfila.com. Ⓜ Alonso Martínez. Transport yourself back in time at this exclusive boutique hotel housed in a beautiful nineteenth-century mansion on a quiet street north of Alonso Martínez. Twelve of the exquisite rooms are suites, there is an elegant terrace for tea and drinks, and an upmarket restaurant run by Michelin-star chef Mario Sandoval. €€€€

HOTEL SANTO MAURO MAP PAGE 92, POCKET MAP H1. C/Zurbano 36 ⓦ marriott. com. Ⓜ Rubén Darío. This is where the Beckhams first installed themselves when David signed for Real Madrid in 2003. A former aristocrat's residence, the hotel has all the luxury and exclusivity you'd expect. Palatial rooms, a restaurant that looks like a gentleman's club, a delightful outdoor terrace and an indoor pool are all part of the package. €€€€

HOTEL ÚNICO MAP PAGE 92, POCKET MAP J2. C/Claudio Cuello 67 Ⓦ unicohotelmadrid.com. Ⓜ Serrano.

Luxury 44-room boutique-style hotel in a renovated nineteenth-century mansion. Large rooms, bathrooms with power showers, elegant communal areas and a garden terrace. The restaurant (see page 98) is run by distinguished Catalan chef Ramón Freixa. €€€€

VELÁZQUEZ 45 BY PILLOW MAP PAGE 92, POCKET MAP K2. C/Velázquez 45, 5° Ⓦ bypillow.com. Ⓜ Velázquez.

Revamped by new owners and converted into a chic *hostal* with smart en-suite rooms, this is a reasonably priced option in an upmarket area of town. €€

Plaza de España

HOSTAL BUENOS AIRES MAP PAGE 102, POCKET MAP D4. Gran Vía 61, 2° Ⓦ hostalbuenosaires-madrid.com. Ⓜ Plaza de España.

Twenty-five pleasantly decorated but small rooms with modern bathrooms, plus double glazing to keep out much of the noise. €

CASÓN DEL TORMES MAP PAGE 102, POCKET MAP C4. C/Río 7 Ⓦ hotelcason deltormes.com. Ⓜ Plaza de España.

Welcoming three-star place in a quiet street next to Plaza de España. The 63 en-suite rooms are functional but very comfortable and hotel facilities include a bar and

breakfast room, and helpful staff. €€

HOTEL EMPERADOR MAP PAGE 102, POCKET MAP D4. Gran Vía 53 Ⓦ emperadorhotel.com. Ⓜ Santo Domingo.

The main reason to come here is the stunning rooftop swimming pool and cocktail bar with its magnificent views. The hotel itself is geared up for the organized tour market and is rather impersonal, but the rooms are large and well decorated. €€€

HOTEL INDIGO MAP PAGE 102, POCKET MAP B1. C/Marqués de Urquijo 4 Ⓦ ihg. com/hotelindigo. Ⓜ Argüelles.

A good option if you are travelling with young children, the *Indigo* provides family rooms with a sofa bed, and the hotel is close to the Parque del Oeste and the *teleférico* into Casa de Campo. €€€

HOTEL SANTO DOMINGO MAP PAGE 102, POCKET MAP D4. C/San Bernardo 1 Ⓦ hotelsantodomingo.es. Ⓜ Santo Domingo.

What with the jungle paintings adorning the car park, the private art collection, the hanging garden and the small rooftop swimming pool and bar with views over the city, this hotel is full of surprises. Rooms have tasteful individual decor, large beds and walk-in shower rooms. €€

HOTEL VP PLAZA ESPAÑA DESIGN MAP PAGE 102, POCKET MAP C3. Ⓦ plazaespana-hotel.com. Ⓜ Plaza España.

Large five-star luxury hotel right on the plaza with 214 spacious rooms, some of which have views over the plaza. It has a small spa, pool and the fashionable *Ginkgo* rooftop bar (see page 111). €€€€

ESSENTIALS

Gran Vía metro station

Arrival

Whatever your point of arrival, it's an easy business getting into the centre of Madrid. The airport is connected by metro, train, shuttle buses and taxis, while the city's main train and bus stations are all linked to the metro system.

By plane

The **Aeropuerto Adolfo Suárez Madrid-Barajas** (ⓦ aena.es) is 16km east of the city. It has four terminals, including the vast T4 building designed by Richard Rogers and Carlos Lamela. T4, a 10min shuttle bus ride from the other terminals, handles all Iberia's domestic and international flights, plus Aer Lingus and airlines that belong to the Oneworld group, such as British Airways and American Airlines; budget airlines, including Easyjet and Ryanair, use T1, while Air France, KLM, ITA and Lufthansa use T2.

From the airport, the **metro link** (Line 8) takes you from T4 and T2 to the city's Nuevos Ministerios station in around twenty minutes (daily 6am–2am; €2.50 for the *tarjeta multi* transport card then €3 supplement plus €1.50 or €8.40 for a one-day *billete turístico*). From there, connecting metro lines take you to city-centre locations in about fifteen minutes. The Cercanías train line takes you directly from T4 to Chamartín in the north of the city in twelve minutes or to Atocha in the south in 25 (daily 6am–11.30pm; €2.60).The route by road to central Madrid is variable, depending on rush-hour traffic, and can take anything from twenty minutes to an hour. Airport express buses run round the clock from each terminal to Cibeles and Atocha (stops only at Cibeles from 11.30pm–6am; every 15–35min; €5)

with a journey time of around forty minutes. Taxis are always available outside, too, and cost €30 to the centre (fixed tariff).

By train

Trains from France and northern Spain (including the high-speed links to Segovia, Valladolid, León, Oviedo and Santiago de Compostela) arrive at the **Estación de Chamartín**, in the north of the city, connected by metro with the centre, and by regular commuter trains (*trenes de cercanías*) to the more central **Estación de Atocha**. Atocha has two interconnected terminals: one for local services; the other for all points in southern and eastern Spain, including the high-speed services to Barcelona, Córdoba, Seville, Toledo, Málaga, Valencia, Alicante, Albacete and Zaragoza. For train information and **reservations**, go to ⓦ renfe.com.

By bus

Bus terminals are scattered throughout the city, but the largest – used by all of the international bus services – is the **Estación Sur de Autobuses** at C/Méndez Álvaro 83, 1.5km south of Atocha train station (ⓦ estacionsurmadrid. avanzagrupo.com, ⓜ Méndez Álvaro).

By car

Although you can access the outer areas of the city by car, there are restrictions about entering the centre (known as *Distrito Centro*) without authorisation. Guests of hotels with carparks in this area can access these as long as their registration is put into the local council system (check with your hotel beforehand).

Getting around

Madrid is an easy city to get around. The central areas are walkable and going on foot is certainly the best way to appreciate and get to know the city. The metro is clean, modern and efficient; buses are also generally very good and serve some of the more out-of-the-way districts, while taxis are always available.

The metro

The **metro** (ⓦ metromadrid.es) is by far the quickest way of getting around Madrid, serving most places you're likely to want to get to. It runs from 6am until 2am and the fare is €1.50–2 for the central zone stations or €12.20 for a ten-trip ticket (*bono de diez viajes*) which can be used on buses too. The metro now operates a paperless ticketing system so you will have to purchase a *tarjeta multi* transport card for €2.50 and then load up the card with the trips you want to take. Alternatively buy a tourist travel pass (see box).

The network has undergone massive expansion in recent years and some of the outlying commuter districts are now connected by light railways which link with the existing metro stations (supplement fares for some of these). Lines are numbered and colour-coded, and the direction of travel is indicated by the name of the terminus station. You can pick up a free colour map of the system (*plano del metro*) at any station.

Local trains

The **local train** network, or *cercanías*, is the most efficient way of connecting between the main train stations and also provides the best route out to many of the suburbs and nearby towns. Most trains are air conditioned, fares are cheap and there are good connections with the metro. Services generally run every fifteen to thirty minutes from 6am to around midnight. For more

Tourist travel pass and the Madrid City Card

If you're using public transport extensively, it's worth thinking about getting a **tourist pass** (*tarjeta turístico*) covering the metro, train and bus. These are non-transferable and you'll need to show your passport or identity card at the time of purchase. Zone A cards cover the city of Madrid, Zone T cards cover the whole region including Toledo and Guadalajara but not the airport buses. They are available for a duration of one to seven days and range in cost from €8.40 for a Zone A daily card to €70.80 for a weekly one for Zone T (under-11s are half price, under-4s are free) and can be purchased at all metro stations, the airport and tourist offices. If you are staying longer, passes (*abonos*) covering the metro, train and bus are available for a calendar month.

Another option worth considering if you want to make the most of your visit to the Spanish capital is the **Madrid City card** (ⓦ citycard.esmadrid.com). The pass gives you discounts on some of the top sights, including the big three art museums and other attractions, and it also includes a Zone A tourist travel pass. A one-day pass costs €8.40, two days €14.20 and you can buy cards for up to five days (children aged 4–11 get a 50% reduction).

information, go to the RENFE website (ⓦrenfe.com) and click on the *cercanías* section for Madrid.

Buses

The comprehensive **bus network** (ⓦemtmadrid.es) is a good way to get around and see the sights. There are information booths at Plaza de Cibeles and Puerta del Sol, which dispense a huge route map (*plano de los transportes de Madrid*) and also sell bus passes, while the EMT Madrid app has all the information you need. Fares are similar to the metro, at €1.50 a journey, or €12.20 for a ten-trip ticket (*bono de diez viajes*) and the *tarjeta multi* (see above in section on the metro) can be used on both forms of transport, but note that you can only buy the single tickets on the buses themselves (try to have the right money to hand).

Services run from 6am to midnight, with *búho* (owl) buses operating through the night on twenty routes around the central area and out to the suburbs: departures are half-hourly midnight–5.30am from Plaza de Cibeles.

Taxis

Madrid has thousands of reasonably priced taxis that you can wave down on the street – look for white cars with a diagonal red stripe on the side. Ride-hailing companies like Cabify, Bolt and Uber also operate in Madrid. Eight to ten euros will get you to most places within the centre and, although it's common to round up the fare, you're not expected to tip. The minimum fare for official taxis is €2.50 (€3.15 on Saturdays, Sundays and holidays) and supplements are charged for going to or from train and bus stations, and outside the city limits. The official Madrid taxi app is known as TxMad. For wheelchair-friendly cabs known as Eurotaxis call ☎915 478 200.

Bicycles

Traditionally a nightmare for cyclists, Madrid has become a marginally more bike-friendly city with the re-introduction of a bicycle hire scheme known as BiciMAD (ⓦbicimad.com). This allows you to pick up and return an electric-assisted bike at stations scattered all over the city centre (€2 for the first hour, €4 for each subsequent hour; minimum age 14).

Useful bus routes

#2 From west to east: from Argüelles metro station running along C/Princesa, past Plaza de España, along Gran Vía, past Cibeles and out past the Retiro.

#3 From south to north: Puerta de Toledo, through Plaza de España, up towards Gran Vía and then Alonso Martínez and northwards.

#5 From Sol via Cibeles, Colón and the Paseo de la Castellana to Chamartín.

#27 From Embajadores, via Atocha, up the length of the Castellana to Plaza de Castilla.

#33 From Príncipe Pío out via the Puente de Segovia to the Parque de Atracciones and Zoo in Casa de Campo.

#C1 and C2 The Circular bus route takes a broad circuit round the city from Atocha, via Puerta de Toledo, Príncipe Pío, Plaza de España, Moncloa, Cuatro Caminos, Avenida de América and Goya.

City tours

The *oficina de turismo* in Plaza Mayor (see page 143) can supply details of guided **English-language walking tours**. Additionally, their website (Ⓦ esmadrid.com/visitas-guiadas-por-madrid) has a list of the companies that run different tours around the city, which usually cost around €10. The website Ⓦ freetour.com offers a host of themed walking tours around the centre, most of which operate on a tip basis. For a **bus tour** of all the major sights, hop on a Madrid City Tour bus at the stop between the Prado and the *Ritz* hotel; tickets cost €22.50 (children & pensioners €11, under-6s free; Ⓦ madrid.city-tour.com) and allow you to jump on and off at various points throughout the city. Pick-up points include Plaza de Colón, Gran Vía, Plaza de España and the Jardín Botánico. Eco TukTuk (Ⓦ ecotuktuk.com) run various tours in electric vehicles with prices starting at €79 for an hour tour for a group of four. For the more adventurous, a number of companies offer **segway tours** of the city with prices starting at €29 for an hour-long tour (Ⓦ madrid-segway.es; Ⓦ segwaytrip.com). Foodies should try Gourmet Madrid Tours (Ⓦ gourmetmadrid.com) to explore the city's culinary highlights

Be aware that it is compulsory for under-16s to wear helmets and that the cycle lanes are also used by cars, though they are supposed to adjust their speed to that of the bicycles.

For bike rentals and tours in and around Madrid, get in touch with Ⓦ bravobike.com at C/Juan Alvarez Mendizábal 19 (Ⓜ Ventura Rodríguez), Ⓦ bikespain.com at Plaza de la Villa 1 (Ⓜ Ópera), Ⓦ trixi.com at C/Jardines 12 (Ⓜ Sol or Gran Vía) and Ⓦ rentandrollmadrid.com at C/Felipe IV 10 (Ⓜ Retiro). All have both conventional and electric bikes.

Car rental

Major operators have branches at the airport and train stations. Central offices include: Avis, Gran Vía 46 (Ⓦ avisworld.com Ⓜ Callao), while Enterprise (Ⓦ enterprise.es), Europcar (Ⓦ europcar.com), Hertz (Ⓦ hertz.com) and Sixt (Ⓦ sixt.es) all have offices at or near Atocha station. Zity (Ⓦ zitycar.es) and Share Now (Ⓦ share-now.com) run electric car sharing schemes in the city centre, and their vehicles can be reserved through their mobile apps, though you will need a driving licence from an EU or EEA country. For more information on driving in Madrid, see page 136.

Directory A-Z

Accessible Travel

Madrid is slowly getting geared up for disabled visitors (*discapacitados*). The local authority has produced a guide with some practical advice at Ⓦ esmadrid.com/en/accessible-madrid. The Organizacíon Nacional de Ciegos de España (ONCE; National Organization for the Blind), C/Prim 3 (Ⓦ once.es; Ⓜ Chueca) provides specialist advice, as does the Federación de Asociaciones de Minusválidos Físicos de la Comunidad de Madrid (FAMMA) at C/Galileo 69 (Ⓞ 915 933 550, Ⓦ famma.org; Ⓜ Islas Filipinas). Wheelchair-accessible taxis can be ordered from Eurotaxi (☎ 665 547 541; ⊜ eurotaxi-madrid.com) or Radio Taxi (☎ 915 478 200; or via email at ⊜ central@rttm.es).

Addresses

Calle (street) is abbreviated to C/ in addresses, followed by the number on the street, then another number that indicates the floor, eg C/Arenal 23, 5˚ means fifth floor of no. 23 Arenal Street. You may also see *izquierda* (*izda*) and *derecha* (*dcha*), meaning (apartment or office) left or right of the staircase.

Cinema

Madrileños love going to the cinema (*cine*), and though most foreign films are dubbed into Spanish, a number of cinemas have original-language screenings, listed in a separate *subtitulada/versión original* (v.o.) section in the newspapers. Tickets cost around €9 but most cinemas have a *día del espectador* (usually Mon or Wed) with a reduced admission charge. Be warned that on Sunday night what seems like half of Madrid goes to the movies and queues can be long. The most central cinemas showing v.o. films include the two Renoirs (⊜ cinesrenoir.com) at C/Martín de los Heros 12 and C/Princesa 5, and Golem (⊜ golem.es) at C/Martín de los Heros 14, all next to Plaza de España, and the nine-screen Ideal Yelmo Complex, C/Doctor Cortezo 6, south off C/Atocha and near Plaza Santa Ana (⊜ yelmocines.es ⊜ Sol).

Crime

Central Madrid is so densely populated – and so busy at just about every hour of the day and night – that it seems to carry very little "big city" threat. However, that's not to say that crime is not a problem, nor that there aren't any sleazy areas to be avoided. Tourists in Madrid, as everywhere, are prime targets for pickpockets and petty thieves, so take care of belongings in crowded areas, on buses, in the metro, burger bars and in the Rastro. Be aware also that although the city council has taken steps to combat the problem, the main routes through Casa de Campo and the Parque del Oeste are still frequented by prostitutes and are best steered clear of at night. Calle Montera, near Sol, and some streets just north of Gran Vía are also affected. To report a crime go to the nearest police station or ring ☎ 901 102 112 (service for foreign tourists; Mon–Fri 9am–9pm; ⊜ bit.ly/SpanishPolice) or ring ☎ 112 or 091 if it is an emergency.

Electricity

The current in Spain is 220v – bring an adaptor (and transformer) to use UK and US laptops, mobile phone chargers, and other electronic devices. Plugs are of the two-prong, round-pin standard European type.

Embassies and consulates

Australia, Torre Espacio, Paseo de la Castellana 259D (☎ 913 536 600, ⊜ spain.embassy.gov.au; ⊜ Begoña); Canada, Torre Espacio, Paseo de la Castellana 259D (☎ 913 828 400, ⊜ canadainternational.gc.ca; ⊜ Begoña); Ireland, Paseo de la Castellana 46, 4˚ (☎ 914 364 093, ⊜ dfa.ie/irish-embassy/spain; ⊜ Rubén Darío); New Zealand, C/Pinar 7, 3˚ (☎ 915 230 226, ⊜ bit.ly/NZMadrid; ⊜ Gregorio Marañón); UK, Torre Espacio, Paseo de la Castellana 259D (☎ 917 146 300 ⊜ gov.uk/government/world/spain; ⊜ Begoña); US, C/Serrano 75 (☎ 915 872 200, ⊜ es.usembassy.gov; ⊜ Rubén Darío); South Africa, C/Claudio Coello 91 (☎ 914 363 780, ⊜ dirco.gov.za/madrid/en; ⊜ Rubén Darío).

Health

EU citizens are entitled to health care free of charge, but ensure you have a European Health Insurance Card. If you are a non-EU citizen, ensure you have health insurance as you may be liable for the costs of any treatment. Following the UK's departure from the EU, its citizens must apply for a Global Health Insurance Card (GHIC), available from: ⓦ bit.ly/GHICCard. Despite the reciprocal arrangement afforded by this system, some form of private medical insurance is recommended.

Health centres are scattered throughout the city and open 24 hours: one of the most central is at Carrera San Jerónimo 32 (ⓣ 913 690 491; ⓜ Sol). Central hospitals include El Clínico San Carlos, C/Profesor Martín Lagos s/n (ⓣ 913 303 000; ⓜ Islas Filipinas); Hospital Gregorio Marañón, C/Dr Esquerdo 46 (ⓣ 915 868 000; ⓜ O'Donnell); Ciudad Sanitaria La Paz, Paseo de la Castellana 261 (ⓣ 917 277 000; ⓜ Begoña). Many doctors speak English, but the Anglo-American Medical Unit is a private English-speaking clinic at C/Conde de Aranda 1 (ⓣ 914 351 823; ⓦ unidadmedica.com; Mon–Fri 9am–8pm, Sat 10am–1pm, August Mon–Fri 10am–5pm, Sat 10am–1pm; ⓜ Retiro). The Clinica Dental Plaza Prosperidad at Plaza Prosperidad 3, 2ºB (ⓣ 914 158 197; ⓦ clinicadentalplazaprosperidad. com; ⓜ Prosperidad) has some English-speaking dentists, as does the Clinica Dental Cisne at C/Magallanes 18 (ⓣ 914 463 221; ⓦ cisnedental. com; ⓜ Quevedo). The following **pharmacies** (distinguished by a green cross) are open 24 hours: C/Mayor 13 (ⓜ Sol); C/Toledo 46 (ⓜ La Latina); C/Atocha 46 (ⓜ Antón Martín); C/Goya 12 (ⓜ Serrano).

Internet

There are free wi-fi hotspots at many newspaper stands in the city and on buses, while most *hostales* and hotels have free wi-fi. The tourist offices in Plaza Mayor and in the Palacio de Cibeles offer free internet while there are free wi-fi hotspots in Plaza Mayor, Plaza Olavide, Plaza Santo Domingo and Plaza Callao.

Left luggage

There are left-luggage facilities (*consignas*) at Barajas Airport in terminals 1 and 4 (both daily 5am–11pm) and 2 (daily 8am–8pm); the Estación Sur bus station (daily 5am–1.30am); and lockers at Atocha (Mon–Fri 5.30am–10.20pm, Sat 6.15am–10.20pm, Sun 6.30am–10.20pm) and Chamartín (open 7am–11pm) train stations. There are also reservable left-luggage services run by ⓦ lockandbefree. com at several locations in the city centre.

LGBTQ+ travellers

The main gay organization in Madrid is Coordinadora Gay de Madrid, C/Puebla 9 (Mon–Thurs 9–2pm & 4–8pm, Fri 9–2pm & 5–8pm; ⓦ cogam.org; ⓜ Gran Vía), which can give information on health, leisure and gay rights. The national LGBTQ+ group can be found nearby at C/Infantas 40, 4º izda (Mon–Fri 8am–3.30pm; ⓦ felgtb. org; ⓜ Banco de España or Chueca). For a good one-stop shop with lots of info on the gay scene, try Berkana Bookshop, C/Hortaleza 62 (Mon–Sat 10.30am–9pm, Sun noon–2pm & 5–9pm; ⓦ libreriaberkana.com; ⓜ Chueca). The website ⓦ shangay. com has listings and information about upcoming events.

Lost property

For lost property, ring the municipal depot on ⓣ 915 279 590 at Paseo del Molino 7 (open Mon–Fri 8.30am–2pm; ⓜ Legazpi), and bring ID. For property left on the metro call ⓣ 900 444 404, on the bus call ☎ 914 068 810, and on local trains ☎ 915 066 969.

Money

Banks are plentiful throughout the city and are the best places to change money. Opening hours are normally Mon–Fri 8.30am–2pm and Thurs 4.30–6.30pm. Branches of El Corte Inglés have exchange offices with long hours and reasonably competitive rates; the most central is on C/Preciados, close to Puerta del Sol. Barajas Airport also has a 24-hour currency exchange office. The rates at the exchange bureaux scattered around the city are often very poor, though they don't usually charge commission. ATM cash machines (*cajeros automáticos*) are widespread and accept most credit and debit cards. Credit cards are widely accepted in hotels, restaurants and shops.

Opening hours

Smaller shops generally open 10am–2pm and 5–8pm Mon–Fri, but only open in the mornings on Sat. Department stores and chains in the tourist zones in the centre tend not to close for lunch and also open all day Sat and Sun. Restaurants generally serve from 1.30–4pm and 8.30–11.30pm, with many closing on Mon. Bars stay open till the early hours – usually around 2am – while clubs close around 5am, depending on the licence they hold. Museums close on Jan 1, Jan 6, May 1, Dec 24, Dec 25 and Dec 31.

Phones

Most mobile phone users should be able to use their phones in Spain – check with your service provider before leaving about costs. However, many American cellphones do not work with the Spanish mobile network. Calling Madrid from abroad, dial your international access code, then 34, followed by the subscriber's number which will nearly always start with 91. For national directory enquiries, ring ☎ 11818; for international enquiries, call ☎ 11825.

Post offices

Centrally located post offices are at Paseo del Prado 1 and in El Corte Inglés, C/Preciados 3 (Ⓜ Sol) and there's another with extended hours at C/Mejía Lequerica 7 (Ⓜ Alonso Martínez). Buy stamps (*sellos*) at *estancos*.

Public holidays

The main national holidays are: Jan 1 (Año Nuevo); Jan 6 (Reyes); Easter Thursday (Jueves Santo); Good Friday (Viernes Santo); May 1 (Fiesta del Trabajo); May 2 (Día de la Comunidad); May 15 (San Isidro); Aug 15 (Virgen de la Paloma); Oct 12 (Día de la Hispanidad); Nov 1 (Todos Los Santos); Nov 9 (Virgen de la Almudena); Dec 6 (Día de la Constitución); Dec 8 (La Inmaculada); Dec 25 (Navidad).

Smoking

Smoking is banned in all bars, restaurants and clubs, though it is common on outdoor terrazas.

Eating out price codes

The price codes used throughout this guide generally refer to two courses plus one drink, plus service, for one person:

€	€20–30
€€	€30–40
€€€	€40–50
€€€€	€50+

Madrid apps

There are a number of apps for phones and tablets which visitors may find useful. The Prado, Thyssen and Reina Sofía all produce guide apps, while the local authority markets the Essential Art Walk Guide app and a 5-D guide to the city. The Metro de Madrid, the city transport agency, the EMT, Taxi Madrid and the BiciMAD bike hire scheme all have their own apps that are available on the Apple Store or Google Play and can be quite helpful in getting around the city.

Swimming pools and aquapark

The Piscina Canal Isabel II, Avda de Filipinas 54 (daily 11am–8pm; ⓜ Ríos Rosas), is a large outdoor swimming pool, and the best central option. Alternatively, try the open-air *piscinas* at Casa de Campo (daily 10am–3pm & 4–9pm; ⓜ Lago) or the Centro Deportivo Municipal José María Cagigal at Calle Santa Pola 22 (daily 10am–3pm & 4–9pm; ⓜ Príncipe Pío or buses #41, #46 and #75). There is an aquapark outside the city in Villanueva de la Cañada (ⓦ villanueva.aquopolis. es), 35km to the west of the city (bus #627, from the *intercambiador* at Moncloa). Outside mid-May to early Sept, most outdoor pools are closed.

Ticket agencies

For theatre and concert tickets, try: ⓦ entradas.com; El Corte Inglés ⓦ elcorteingles.es/entradas; ⓦ ticketea.com; and Ticketmaster ⓦ ticketmaster.es. The website ⓦ atrapalo.com also sells discount tickets for the theatre and musicals.

Time

Madrid is one hour ahead of Greenwich Mean Time during winter and two hours ahead from March–October. Clocks go forward an hour in late March and back in late October.

Tipping

When tipping, adding around five to ten percent to a restaurant bill is acceptable, but rarely more than €5, while in bars and taxis, rounding up to the nearest euro is the norm.

Tourist information

The chief tourist offices are at the following locations: Barajas International Airport T1, T2 & T4; T1 (Mon–Sat 9am–8pm, Sun 9am–2pm; ☎ 913 058 656); T2 (daily 9.30am–8.30pm; ☎ 915 787 810); T4 (daily 9.30am–8.30pm; ☎ 915 787 810); CentroCentro in the Palacio de Cibeles (Tues–Sun 10am–8pm; ☎ 915 787 810; ⓜ Banco de España); Estación de Atocha (Mon–Fri 9am–8pm, Sat 8am–3pm, Sun 9am–2pm; ☎ 915 284 630; ⓜ Atocha Renfe); Plaza Mayor 27 (daily 9.30am–8.30pm; ☎ 915 787 810; ⓜ Sol). These are supplemented by booths near the Palacio Real, the Prado, the Reina Sofia and in Plaza del Callao off Gran Vía (daily 9.30am–8.30pm). The Madrid tourist board has a comprehensive website at ⓦ esmadrid.com, while the regional one covers the whole of the province at ⓦ turismomadrid.es/en. You can phone for tourist information in English on ☎ 902 100 007, a premium-rate number that links all the regional

Emergency numbers

For the police, medical services and the fire brigade, call ☎ 112.

tourist offices mentioned below, and on ☎ 915 881 636.

Listings information is in plentiful supply in Madrid. Spanish website *La Guía del Ocio* (🌐 guiadelocio.es) has extensive information on museums, exhibitions, bars, restaurants and nightlife. The *ayuntamiento* (city council) also publishes a monthly what's-on magazine, *esMadrid* (in English and Spanish), free from any of the tourist offices. Finally, 🌐 nakedmadrid.com and 🌐 madridnofrills.com are English-language websites that feature useful reviews of bars and restaurants, and articles about the city.

Theatre

Madrid has a vibrant theatre scene which, if you speak the language, is worth sampling. You can catch anything from Lope de Vega to contemporary productions, and there's a good range on offer during the annual Festival de Otoño (Nov–Dec). For current productions, check the listings sources above.

Travelling with children

Children are doted on in Spain and welcome in nearly all cafés and restaurants. Although many of Madrid's main sights may lack children-specific activities, there's still plenty to keep kids occupied during a short stay, from various parks – including the Retiro (see page 70) – to swimming pools (see page 143) and the zoo (see page 106). There is also an ecological theme park/zoo on the outskirts of the city (🌐 faunia.es).

Festivals and events

As well as these festivals, check out the **cultural events** organized by the city council, in particular the Veranos de la Villa (July–Sept) and Festival de Otoño a Primavera (Nov–June), which include music concerts, theatre and cinema. There are annual festivals for flamenco (May), books (end of May to early June), dance (May–June), photography (June–Aug) and jazz (Nov). See 🌐 esmadrid.com.

Cabalgata de los Reyes

January 5
To celebrate the arrival of the gift-bearing Three Kings, there is a gigantic, hugely popular evening procession through the city centre in which children are showered with sweets. It's held on the evening before presents are traditionally exchanged in Spain.

Carnaval

The week before Lent
Partying and fancy-dress parades, especially in the gay zone around Chueca. The end of Carnaval is marked by the bizarre parade, El Entierro de la Sardina (The Burial of the Sardine), on Paseo de la Florida.

Semana Santa

Easter week is celebrated with a series of solemn processions around Madrid, with Jueves Santo (Maundy Thursday) and Viernes Santo (Good Friday) both public holidays in the city.

Fiesta del Dos de Mayo

May 2
Celebrations are held around Madrid to commemorate the city's uprising against the French in 1808.

Fiestas de San Isidro

May 15, for a week
Evenings start out with traditional *chotis*, music and dancing, and bands play each night in the Jardines de las Vistillas (south of the Palacio Real). The fiestas mark the start of the bullfighting season.

La Feria del Libro

End of May
Madrid's great book fair takes place with stands set up in Retiro Park.

WorldPride Madrid

End of June or beginning of July
WorldPride Madrid (LGTBQ+ Pride Week) is a week-long party in Chueca culminating in a parade that brings the city centre to a standstill.

Castizo fiestas

August 6 to 15
Madrileños put on traditional fiestas to celebrate the saints' days of San Cayetano, San Lorenzo and La Virgen de la Paloma. Much of the activity centres around C/Toledo, Plaza de la Paja and the Jardines de las Vistillas.

Navidad

The Christmas period in Madrid sees Plaza Mayor taken over by a model of a Nativity crib and a large seasonal market with stalls selling all manner of festive decorations.

Noche Vieja

Dec 31
Puerta del Sol is the customary place to gather for midnight, waiting for the strokes of the clock and then attempting to swallow a grape on each strike to bring good luck in the coming year.

Chronology

800s Muslims establish a defensive outpost on the escarpment above the Manzanares river. It becomes known as "mayrit" – the place of many springs – successively modified to Magerit and then Madrid.

1086 Madrid taken by the Christians under Alfonso VI, but it remains a relatively insignificant backwater.

1561 Felipe II chooses Madrid as a permanent home for the court because of its position in the centre of the recently unified Spain. The population surges with the arrival of the royal entourage, and there is a boom in the building industry.

1700–46 With the emergence of the Bourbon dynasty under Felipe V, a touch of French style, including the sumptuous Palacio Real, is introduced into the capital.

1759–88 Carlos III tries to make the city into a home worthy of the monarchy. Streets are cleaned up, sewers and street lighting installed, and work begins on the Museo del Prado.

1795–1808 Spain falls under the influence of Napoleonic France, with their troops entering the capital in 1808. The heavily out-gunned *madrileños* are defeated in a rising on May 2 and Napoleon installs his brother Joseph on the throne.

1812–14 The French are removed by a combined Spanish and British army and the monarchy makes a return under the reactionary Fernando VII.

1833–75 Spanish society is riven with divisions which explode into a series of conflicts known as the Carlist Wars and lead to chronic political instability, including a brief period as a republic.

1875–1900 Madrid undergoes significant social changes prompted by a rapid growth in population and the emergence of a working class. The socialist party, the PSOE, is founded in the city in 1879.

1923–31 A hard-line military regime under Miguel Primo de Rivera takes control, with King Alfonso XIII relegated to the background. The king eventually decides to abdicate in 1931, and the Second Republic is ushered in.

1936–39 The Right grows increasingly restless and a group of army generals organize an uprising in July 1936 which ignites the Spanish Civil War. Madrid resists and becomes a Republican stronghold.

1939 Franco and his victorious Nationalists enter the city. Mass reprisals take place and Franco installs himself in the country residence of El Pardo.

1939–53 Spain endures yet more suffering during the post-war years until a turnaround in American policy. The Pact of Madrid is signed to rehabilitate Franco, as the US searches for anti-Communist Cold War allies.

1970s Franco eventually dies in November 1975. He is succeeded by King Juan Carlos who presides over the transition to democracy.

1981 In a last-gasp attempt to re-establish itself, the military under Colonel Tejero storms the parliament in Madrid, but a lack of support from the king and army causes its collapse. The Socialists led by Felipe González win the 1982 elections.

1980s Freedom from the shackles of dictatorship and the release of long-pent-up creative forces help create La Movida, with Madrid becoming the epicentre of the movement.

1990s The Socialists become increasingly discredited as they are entangled in a web of scandal and corruption, losing control of Madrid in

1991 and the country in 1996 to the conservative Partido Popular (PP).

1992 Madrid is named European Capital of Culture.

2004 The March 11 bombings carried out by Muslim extremists at Atocha train station kill 191 and injure close to 2000. The Socialists return to power in the general elections which follow, although the PP remain firmly in control of the local government.

2004–08 Madrid fails in its bids for the 2012 and 2016 Olympics, losing out to London and then Rio de Janeiro. High-profile building projects such as the Richard Rogers' airport terminal, Norman Foster's Torre Caja Madrid skyscraper, Rafael Moneo's Prado extension and the M30 ring road 6-km long mega-tunnel are all completed before the onset of the recession and the end of the property boom.

2008–13 The effects of the global economic crisis combined with the endemic problems of property speculation, profligate spending on showcase projects and corruption mean the crisis hits Spain even harder. The centre-right Popular Party is returned to power in the 2011 general election. Unemployment reaches record highs, the economy flatlines in terms of growth and corruption scandals continue to plague the country.

2014 Juan Carlos abdicates after nearly forty years on the throne. His son Felipe succeeds as King of Spain.

2015 Support for the Popular Party plummets and the left-of-centre citizen-based Ahora Madrid group, led by mayor Manuela Carmena, come to power in 2015. They pick up the pieces and try to get to grips with the problems of corruption and debt bequeathed by the PP, whilst dealing with the high levels of pollution with the introduction of a low-emissions zone in the city centre.

2019–23 The Popular Party tighten their grip on the local and regional government in the 2023 elections despite criticism of their handling of the Covid-19 pandemic and the creeping privatisation of the health service. They recapture control of the Madrid city council after doing a deal with the right-leaning Ciudadanos party and far-right Vox group, despite their worst ever showing in the local elections in the capital. They pledge to roll back Carmena's reforms, prompting protests from residents and environmental groups.

Spanish

Once you get into it, Spanish is one of the easiest languages around, and people are eager to try and understand even the most faltering attempt. English is spoken at the main tourist attractions, but you'll get a far better reception if you try communicating with *madrileños* in their own tongue.

Pronunciation
The rules of pronunciation are pretty straightforward and strictly observed.

A somewhere between the A sound of back and that of father.

E as in get.

I as in police.

O as in hot.

U as in rule.

C is spoken like a TH before E and I, hard otherwise: *cerca* is pronounced "therka".

G is a guttural H sound (like the ch in loch) before E or I, a hard G elsewhere – *gigante* becomes "higante".

H is always silent.

J is the same as a guttural G: *jamón* is "hamon".

LL sounds like an English Y: *tortilla* is pronounced "torteeya".

N is as in English unless it has a tilde (accent) over it, when it becomes NY: *mañana* sounds like "manyana".

QU is pronounced like an English K.

R is rolled when it is at the start of a word, RR doubly so.

V sounds more like B, *vino* becoming "beano".

X has an S sound before consonants, normal X before vowels.

Z is the same as a soft C, so *cerveza* becomes "thairbaytha".

Words and phrases

Basics
yes, no, ok sí, no, vale
please, thank you por favor, gracias
where?, when? ¿dónde?, ¿cuándo?
what?, how much? ¿qué?, ¿cuánto?
Help! ¡socorro!
here, there aquí, allí
this, that esto, eso
now, later ahora, más tarde
open, closed abierto/a, cerrado/a
with, without con, sin
good, bad buen(o)/a, mal(o)/a
big, small gran(de), pequeño/a
cheap, expensive barato, caro
hot, cold caliente, frío
more, less más, menos
today, tomorrow hoy, mañana
yesterday ayer
the bill la cuenta
price precio
free gratis
doctor un médico
police la policía

Greetings and responses
hello, goodbye hola, adiós
good morning buenos días
good afternoon/night buenas tardes/noches
see you later hasta luego

sorry lo siento/disculpe
excuse me con permiso/perdón
How are you? ¿Cómo está (usted)?
I (don't) understand (no) entiendo
not at all/you're welcome de nada
Do you speak english? ¿Habla (usted) inglés?
I (don't) speak Spanish (no) hablo español
My name is... Me llamo...
What's your name? ¿Cómo se llama usted?
I am... Soy...
English inglés(a)
Scottish escocés(a)
Welsh galés(a)
Australian australiano(a)
Canadian canadiense
American americano(a)
Irish irlandés(a)
New Zealander neozelandés(a)

Hotels, transport and directions

I want Quiero
I'd like Quisiera
Do you know...? ¿Sabe....?
I don't know No sé
Give me (one like that) Deme (uno así)
Do you have...? ¿Tiene...?
the time la hora
single room habitación individual
double room habitación doble
two beds/double bed dos camas/cama de matrimonio
with shower/bath con ducha/baño
it's for one person es para una persona
for one night para una noche
for one week para una semana
How do I get to...? ¿Por dónde se va a....?
left, right, straight on izquierda, derecha, todo recto
opposite frente a..
behind detrás de...
in front of enfrente de...
next to al lado de...
Where is the bus station/post office/toilet? ¿Dónde está la estación de autobuses/la oficina de correos/el baño?
What´s this in Spanish? ¿Cómo se dice en español?
Where does the bus to... leave from? ¿De dónde sale el autobús para...?

I'd like a (return) ticket to... Quisiera un billete (de ida y vuelta) para...
What time does it leave? ¿A qué hora sale?
platform el andén
ticket office la taquilla
timetable el horario

Money

How much? ¿Cuánto es?
I would like to change some money Me gustaría cambiar dinero
ATM cash machine cajero automático
foreign exchange bureau la oficina de cambio
credit card tarjeta de crédito
travellers' cheques cheques de viaje

Numbers/days/months/seasons

1 un/uno/una
2 dos
3 tres
4 cuatro
5 cinco
6 seis
7 siete
8 ocho
9 nueve
10 diez
11 once
12 doce
13 trece
14 catorce
15 quince
16 dieciséis
17 diecisiete
18 dieciocho
19 diecinueve
20 veinte
21 veintiuno
30 treinta
40 cuarenta
50 cincuenta
60 sesenta
70 setenta
80 ochenta
90 noventa
100 cien(to)
101 ciento uno
200 doscientos
500 quinientos
1000 mil

Monday lunes
Tuesday martes
Wednesday miércoles
Thursday jueves
Friday viernes
Saturday sábado
Sunday domingo
today hoy
yesterday ayer
tomorrow mañana
January enero
February febrero
March marzo
April abril
May mayo
June junio
July julio
August agosto
September septiembre
October octubre
November noviembre
December diciembre
Spring primavera
Summer verano
Autumn otoño
Winter invierno

Food and drink

Basics

aceite oil
agua water
ajo garlic
arroza rice
azúcar sugar
huevos eggs
mantequilla butter
miel honey
pan bread
pimienta pepper
pinchos/pintxos a small bite-sized tapa
queso cheese
sal salt
sopa soup
tapa small serving of food
vinagre vinegar

Meals

almuerzo/comida lunch
botella bottle

carta menu
cena dinner
comedor dining room
cuchara spoon
cuchillo knife
desayuno breakfast
menú (del día) daily set-lunch
menú de degustación set menu offering a taste of several house specialities
mesa table
platos combinados mixed plate
ración a plateful of food
tenedor fork
vaso glass

Meat

albóndigas meatballs
callos tripe
caracoles snails
chorizo spicy sausage
conejo rabbit
cochinillo roast suckling pig
hígado liver
jamón serrano cured ham
jamón de york regular ham
morcilla black pudding
pollo chicken
salchicha sausage

Seafood

ahumados smoked fish
almejas clams
anchoas anchovies
atún tuna
a la marinera seafood cooked with garlic, onions and white wine
bacalao cod
bonito premium-quality tuna
boquerones small, anchovy-like fish, usually served in vinegar
calamares squid
cangrejo crab
gambas prawns
langostinos langoustines
mejillones mussels
ostras oysters
pulpo octopus

Fruit and vegetables

aceitunas olives

alcachofas artichokes
berenjena aubergine/eggplant
cebolla onion
cerezas cherries
champiñones mushrooms
coliflor cauliflower
ensalada salad
fresa strawberry
garbanzos chickpeas
granada pomegranate
habas broad/fava beans
higos figs
lechuga lettuce
lentejas lentils
limón lemon
manzana apple
melocotones peaches
nabos turnips
naranja orange
pepino cucumber
pimientos peppers
pimientos de padrón small peppers, with the odd hot one thrown in
piña pineapple
pisto assortment of cooked vegetables (like ratatouille)
plátano banana
pomelo grapefruit
puerros leeks
puré thick soup
repollo cabbage
sandía watermelon
setas oyster mushrooms
sopa soup
tomate tomato
uvas grapes
zanahoria carrot

specialities

bocadillo French-loaf sandwich
cocido meat and chickpea stew
croquetas croquettes, with bits of ham in
empanada slices of fish/meat pie

ensaladilla Russian salad (diced vegetables in mayonnaise, often with tuna)
patatas alioli potatoes in garlic mayonnaise
patatas bravas fried potatoes in spicy tomato sauce
tortilla (española) potato omelette
tortilla francesa plain omelette
tostas toasted bread with a topping

Cooking methods

al ajillo with olive oil and garlic
a la parilla charcoal-grilled
a la plancha grilled on a hot plate
a la romana fried in batter
al horno baked in the oven
asado roast
frito fried

Desserts

arroz con leche rice pudding
crema catalana Catalan crème brûlée
cuajada cream-based dessert often served with honey
flan crème caramel
helado ice cream
melocotón en almíbar peaches in syrup
membrillo quince paste
nata whipped cream
natillas custard
yogur yoghurt

Drinks

anís aniseed liqueur
café (con leche) (white) coffee
cerveza beer
té tea
vino wine
...blanco white
...rosado rosé
...tinto red
vermút vermouth
zumo juice

Glossary

alameda park or grassy promenade
alcázar Moorish fortified palace
asador restaurant specialising in roast meats such as lamb

avenida avenue (usually abbreviated to avda)
ayuntamiento town hall or council
azulejo glazed ceramic tilework
barrio suburb or neighbourhood

bodega cellar or wine bar

calle (usually abbreviated to C/) street or road

capilla mayor chapel containing the high altar

capilla real royal chapel

carretera highway

castillo castle

cervecería bar specializing in beer

chotis Madrid's traditional dance

correos post office

corrida bullfight

cuadrilla a bullfighter's team of assistants

edificio building

ermita hermitage

estanco small shop selling stamps and tobacco, recognizable by the brown and yellow signs bearing the word *tabacos*

farmacia pharmacy/chemist

gasolina petrol

iglesia church

judería Jewish quarter

lavabo washbasin, toilet

lonja market

marisquería seafood restaurant

mercado market

mesón an old-style restaurant

mirador viewing point

Movida late Seventies/early Eighties creative explosion in Madrid, viewed as Spain's Swinging Sixties

Mudéjar Muslim Spaniard subject to medieval Christian rule, but retaining Islamic worship; most commonly a term applied to architecture which includes buildings built by Moorish craftsmen for the Christian rulers and later designs influenced by Moors. The 1890s to 1930s saw a Mudéjar revival, blended with Art Nouveau and Art Deco forms

museo museum

oficina de turismo tourist office

palacio aristocratic mansion

parador state-run hotel, usually housed in a building of historic interest

patio inner courtyard

Plateresco/Plateresque an elaborately decorative Renaissance style, the sixteenth-century successor of Isabelline forms. Named for its resemblance to silversmiths' work (*platería*)

plaza square

plaza de toros bullring

posada old name for an inn

puerta gateway

puerto port

servicio toilet

sidrería bar specializing in cider

taberna tavern

tasca old-style bar

terraza summer outdoor bar/terrace

zarzuela light opera

Publishing Information
Fifth edition 2024

Distribution
UK, Ireland and Europe
Apa Publications (UK) Ltd; sales@roughguides.com
United States and Canada
Ingram Publisher Services; ips@ingramcontent.com
Australia and New Zealand
Booktopia; retailer@booktopia.com.au
Worldwide
Apa Publications (UK) Ltd; sales@roughguides.com

Special Sales, Content Licensing and CoPublishing
Rough Guides can be purchased in bulk quantities at discounted prices. We can create special editions, personalised jackets and corporate imprints tailored to your needs. sales@roughguides.com.
roughguides.com

Printed in Czech Republic

This book was produced using **Typefi** automated publishing software.

A catalogue record for this book is available from the British Library

The publishers and authors have done their best to ensure the accuracy and currency of all the information in **Pocket Rough Guide Madrid**, however, they can accept no responsibility for any loss, injury, or inconvenience sustained by any traveller as a result of information or advice contained in the guide.

Rough Guide Credits
Editor: Rachel Lawrence
Cartography: Carte
Picture Editor: Piotr Kala
Picture Manager: Tom Smyth
Layout: Grzegorz Madejak

Original design: Richard Czapnik
Head of DTP and Pre-Press: Rebeka Davies
Head of Publishing: Sarah Clark

Acknowledgements
Thank you to the Metro de Madrid for the use of their underground map.

SMALL PRINT

About the author

Simon Baskett lives and works in Madrid with his wife, Trini, and two children Patrick and Laura. He is a long-suffering Atlético Madrid fan, and has not yet given up hope that he might live long enough to see them win the Champions League. His ambition is to win El Gordo (the huge Christmas lottery) and retire to a local bar.

Help us update

We've gone to a lot of effort to ensure that this edition of the **Pocket Rough Guide Madrid** is accurate and up-to-date. However, things change – places get "discovered", opening hours are notoriously fickle, restaurants and rooms raise prices or lower standards. If you feel we've got it wrong or left something out, we'd like to know, and if you can remember the address, the price, the hours, the phone number, so much the better.

Please send your comments with the subject line "**Pocket Rough Guide Madrid Update**" to mail@uk.roughguides.com. We'll credit all contributions and send a copy of the next edition (or any other Rough Guide if you prefer) for the very best emails.

Photo Credits

(Key: T-top; C-centre; B-bottom; L-left; R-right)

1862 Dry Bar 88
Bodega de los Secretos 75, 76
Lydia Evans/Rough Guides 35, 54, 111
Olga Planas/Ana La Santa 60
Shutterstock 1, 2TL, 2BR, 2BL, 2C, 4, 5, 6, 10, 11B, 11T, 12B, 12/13T, 12/13B, 13C, 14B, 14T, 15B, 15T, 16B, 16T, 17B, 17T, 18T, 18C, 18B, 19T, 19C, 19B, 20T, 20C, 20B, 21T, 21C, 21B, 22C, 22T, 22B, 23T, 23C, 23B, 24/25, 26, 27, 30, 32, 33, 34, 36, 37, 39, 40, 43, 44, 45, 46, 50, 51, 53, 55, 56, 57, 58, 59, 62, 63, 64, 65, 69, 70, 71, 72, 73, 74, 77, 78, 79, 82, 83, 87, 91, 94, 95, 97, 98, 99, 100, 101, 104, 105, 107, 109, 110, 112, 115, 117, 119, 120, 122, 123, 124/125, 134/135
Tim Draper/Rough Guides 61, 84, 96, 106, 108

Cover: Plaza de Cibeles **Sergii Figurnyi/Shutterstock**

Index

RED DE METRO Y METRO LIG

SIMBOLOGÍA *Key*

- Estación accesible / ascensor — *Step-free access / lift*
- Transbordo corto — *Metro interchange*
- Transbordo largo — *Metro interchange with long walking distance*
- Cambio de tren — *Change of trains*
- Metro Ligero — *Light Rail*
- Cercanías — *Suburban railway*
- Autobuses interurbanos — *Suburban buses*
- Autobuses largo recorrido — *Interregional bus station*
- Terminal autobuses nocturnos — *Night bus line terminal*
- Autobús exprés aeropuerto — *Airport express bus*
- Estación de tren — *Railway station*
- Aeropuerto / Airport — Adolfo Suárez Madrid-Barajas

- **ZONA A** / **ZONA B1** Zonas tarifarias — *Fare zones*
- ATENCIÓN A LA TARIFA — Validación a la SALIDA — *PAY THE RIGHT FARE / Ticket checked at the EXIT*
- Atención al cliente — *Customer Service*
- Oficina de gestión — Tarjeta Transporte Público — *Public Transport Card Office*
- Objetos perdidos — *Lost and found*
- **Bibliometro** — *Metro Library*
- Productos oficiales Metro — *Official Metro merchandising*
- Aparcamiento disuasorio gratuito — Free park and ride — *Excepto días con evento / *Except days with event*
- Aparcamiento disuasorio de pago — *Paid park and ride*
- Estacionamiento de bicicletas — *Bicycle parking*

- Espacio histórico de Metro — *Metro historical space*
- Área acceso restringido para vehículos privados — *Area with restricted traffic access*
- Tramo temporalmente cerrado — *Section temporarily closed*

HORARIO *Opening times*

Todos los días de 06:00 a 01:30 h.
Every day from 6:00 a.m. to 1:30 a.m.

Líneas

1. Pinar de Chamartín / Valdecarros
2. Las Rosas / Cuatro Caminos
3. Villaverde Alto / Moncloa
4. Argüelles / Pinar de Chamartín
5. Alameda de Osuna / Casa de Campo
6. Circular
7. Hospital del Henares / Pitis
8. Nuevos Ministerios / Aeropuerto T4
9. Paco de Lucía / Arganda del Rey
10. Hospital Infanta Sofía / Puerta del Sur
11. Plaza Elíptica / La Fortuna
12. MetroSur
R. Ópera / Príncipe Pío

Metro Ligero

1. Pinar de Chamartín / Las Tablas
2. Colonia Jardín / Estación de Aravaca
3. Colonia Jardín / Puerta de Boadilla